D1600665

ROBERT DREWS

BASILEUS

THE EVIDENCE FOR KINGSHIP IN GEOMETRIC GREECE

Yale University Press

New Haven and London

Published with the generous assistance of Vanderbilt University.

Designed by Nancy Ovedovitz and set in Linotron 202 Trump Medieval type by The Composing Room of Michigan.
Printed in the United States of America by
Halliday Lithograph, West Hanover, Mass.

Library of Congress Cataloging in Publication Data

Drews, Robert.
  Basileus: the evidence for kingship in geometric Greece.

  (Yale classical monographs; 4)
  Bibliography: p. 133
  Includes index.
  1. Greece—History—Geometric period, ca. 900–700 B.C. 2. Greece—Kings and rulers. 3. Cities and towns, Ancient—Greece—History. I. Title. II. Series.
DF221.5.D73 1983   938'.01   82–10915
ISBN 0–300–02831–8

10 9 8 7 6 5 4 3 2 1

CONTENTS

ACKNOWLEDGMENTS

In the summer of 1980 I began a study formally titled "the founding of cities in pre-classical antiquity." As background to that study I decided to look closely at what evidence we have about Greek *poleis* during the Geometric period, and thus I became entangled in the subject of this monograph. I should like here to express my appreciation to the John Simon Guggenheim Memorial Foundation for its support and for the grace with which it goes about its business. I also thank Vanderbilt University for making a subvention toward the publication costs of this volume. And finally I am grateful to the Yale University Press and to the Yale Classical Monographs Committee for publishing a book for which, others assure me, the market is small and shrinking.

My colleague William Race assisted me with the manuscript at a critical stage, a kindness deeply appreciated. And I owe much to Professor Chester Starr, from whose personal support I have profited, and whose creative explorations of early Greek history have helped me frequently, even when (as in the present study) my conclusions differ from his.

Translations of Pausanias are taken from the Loeb Classical Library edition prepared by W. H. S. Jones and H. A. Ormerod, and are reprinted here by permission of Harvard University Press. I have used, with adaptations, the translations of A. Lang, W. Leaf, S. Butcher, and E. Myers for the *Iliad* and the *Odyssey*. Other translations, unless noted, are my own. For the photograph of the Arcesilas Cup, and permission to publish it, I thank the Bibliothèque nationale in Paris.

Nashville, Tennessee
March 1982

ABBREVIATIONS

For abbreviations not listed below, see *The Oxford Classical Dictionary*², ed. N. G. L. Hammond and H. H. Scullard (Oxford: Oxford Univ. Press, 1970), pp. ix–xxii.

ABSA	*Annual of the British School at Athens*
AJA	*American Journal of Archaeology*
AJP	*American Journal of Philology*
CIG	*Corpus Inscriptionum Graecarum*
CP	*Classical Philology*
F.Gr.Hist.	F. Jacoby, *Die Fragmente der griechischen Historiker* (Berlin and Leiden, 1923–58)
RE	A. Pauly, G. Wissowa, and W. Kroll, *Real-Encyclopädie der klassischen Altertumswissenschaft* (1893–1978)
REG	*Revue des études grecques*
RH	*Revue historique*

CHAPTER I INTRODUCTION

The Dark Age of Greece, roughly the period that falls between the Linear B tablets of ca. 1200 B.C. and the epics of the eighth century, has begun to come to light. Several books on the period have recently been written by eminent archaeologists, and a dim outline of the material side of Dark Age life is now emerging. The abstract, as usual, trails behind the concrete. The contributions made by archaeologists now invite historians to attend to their part of the picture, and it may be that some basic revisions are imminent.[1]

In our conventional picture of Dark Age Greece, the various and many communities are ruled by kings. We are careful to concede that these kings were not an impressive lot, and that each sought advice and consent from a council of elders. But the form which we describe is nonetheless monarchical.[2]

1. Most important, perhaps, will be a reexamination of the belief that in Dark Age Greece organizations based on family, kin, and clan were more significant than the polis. In *RH* 254 (1975), pp. 286–89, J.-P. Martin summarizes the public defense of what seems to be a convincing thesis, by F. Bourriot, discrediting the *genos* as a general form of social organization in Athens and most other Greek states. I have not seen the thesis, which has been published in a photocopy of the original typescript (in two volumes, 1421 pages): F. Bourriot, "Recherches sur la nature du genos. Étude d'histoire sociale athénienne. Périodes archaïque et classique" (Thèse de Lille; Paris: Champion, 1976). See the review by P. Ducrey in *Museum Helveticum* 34 (1977):263, and the comments of Chester Starr, *The Economic and Social Growth of Early Greece: 800–500 B.C.* (New York: Oxford Univ. Press, 1977), pp. 137–38.

2. Early essays on Greek kingship in the Homeric period tended to focus on Agamemnon; whether there was or was not a king of all Greece, in the Bronze Age, was the central question. That question having been largely settled by the

Our conventional picture is drawn in broad strokes. When filling in details, one is free to choose from a surprising array of possibilities. The time at which kingship gave way to aristocracy, for instance, is placed anywhere from the late ninth to the early seventh century. In his survey of Greek history Hermann Bengtson dates "die Beseitigung der königlichen Gewalt" prior to the beginnings, ca. 750 B.C., of the period of colonization. Chester Starr, believing that some early colonies had kings, dated the disappearance of monarchy to the last decades of the eighth century.[3] In his revision of J. B. Bury's famous history of Greece, Russell Meiggs prefers an earlier date for "the gradual weakening of the king's position and the transfer of his power to the nobility," and suggests that this evolution had in most places taken place "by the end of the ninth century."[4] A recent book by Raphael Sealey extends the transition from monarchy to aristocracy well into the seventh century.[5]

As there are different assumptions about the date of its disappearance, so are there varying opinions about what this thing was that disappeared. When they use the word "king," most historians envisage a monarch of a polis: a king of Corinth, for example, or a king of Miletus. Others, however, have in mind not a king of a polis, but of a *Stammstaat*, a loose coalition of

---

Linear B tablets, interest now focuses on the differences between Mycenaean and post-Mycenaean kings. Among the most important recent studies are: Chester Starr, "The Decline of the Early Greek Kings," *Historia* 10 (1961): 129–38; Pavel Oliva, "ΠΑΤΡΙΚΗ ΒΑΣΙΛΕΙΑ," pp. 171–81 in *Geras: Studies Presented to George Thomson on the Occasion of his 60th Birthday,* ed. L. Varcl and R. F. Willetts (Prague: Charles University, 1963); C. G. Thomas, "The Roots of Homeric Kingship," *Historia* 15 (1966): 387–407; C. G. Thomas, "From Wanax to Basileus: Kingship in the Greek Dark Age," *Hispania Antiqua* 6 (1978):187–206.

3. H. Bengtson, *Griechische Geschichte von den Anfängen bis in die römische Kaiserzeit,* 4th ed. (Munich: Beck, 1969), p. 66; Starr, "Early Greek Kings," pp. 129ff.

4. J. B. Bury and R. Meiggs, *A History of Greece to the Death of Alexander* (New York: St. Martin's, 1975), p. 64.

5. Raphael Sealey, *A History of the Greek City States, 700–338 B.C.* (Berkeley: Univ. of California Press, 1976), p. 24.

peoples who spoke the same dialect, worshipped the same deities, and regarded themselves as kinsmen. A Russian historian, Juri Andreev, has in a recent and stimulating article[6] proposed that a ninth-century *basileus* ruled neither a polis nor a *Stammstaat*, but one of the minuscule entities—a village, for example, or a deme—which in the eighth century would coalesce into a single polis. At that point, Andreev suggests, the kinglets were transformed into aristocrats, exchanging their petty monarchies for places on the aristocratic council.

Our conventional picture, though not in all its variations, is an old one. Not only was it drawn by the early masters of scholarly history, such as George Grote and Ernst Curtius,[7] but one will also find it roughly sketched by Charles Rollin, who early in the eighteenth century moralized about the Greek kings:

The primordial grounds of all those different states was monarchical government, the most ancient of all forms, the most universally received and established, the most proper to maintain peace and concord.

Whereas Grote and Curtius would find the decline of monarchy a happy chapter in Greek history, Rollin saw it as a grim precedent:

But, as the state of things degenerated by degrees, . . . a totally different spirit seized the people, which prevailed all over Greece, kindled a violent desire of liberty, and brought about a general change of government every where, except in Macedonia; so that monarchy gave way to a republican government.[8]

Another major difference between the presentations of

6. Juri Andreev, "Könige und Königsherrschaft in den Epen Homers," *Klio* 61 (1979):361–84.
7. George Grote, *A History of Greece*, 12 vols. (1849; reprint ed., New York: Dutton, 1906), 2:178–82. Ernst Curtius, *The History of Greece*, trans. Adolphus Ward, 5 vols. (New York: Scribner, Armstrong and Co., 1876), 1:150–52, 262–74.
8. Charles Rollin, *Ancient History*, 2 vols. (Glasgow, Edinburgh, and London: Blackie and Son, 1845. Translated from the French edition of 1729), 1:266.

Rollin on the one hand, and George Grote and the scholarly historians on the other, is that the latter were far less confident about the particulars in the Greeks' traditions about their early kings. The legends did not constitute respectable evidence. Grote despaired of recovering events in Greece before the time of Homer (which, for Grote, was the late ninth century), but he did trust that the epics mirrored the conditions of the pre-Homeric world. Hence, though the tales about individual kings had to be discounted, one could still assume that the king was indeed the centerpiece in "the primitive Grecian government."[9] For Georg Busolt, it would appear, the less said about the pre-Homeric kings, the better. In his massive *Griechische Geschichte* a mere seventeen lines describe what that monarchy was like, and how it evolved into an aristocracy.[10] In the twentieth century most historians have, like Busolt, contented themselves with a few generalizations about the kings of the Greek Dark Age, but the old picture is nonetheless still in place.

Yet there are signs of a more basic skepticism. W. G. Forrest's *The Emergence of Greek Democracy* portrays the embryonic polis of 800 B.C. as ruled either by "a king surrounded by an often troublesome aristocracy" or, remarkably, by "aristocrats alone."[11] Lillian Jeffery has recently called attention to the generally shaky character of the traditions about kings in non-Doric Greece.[12] And Andreev not only concludes that aristocracy was the form of government in the typical polis of Homer's own day, but also suggests that genuine monarchy had vanished with the Mycenaean world.[13]

It is time, then, for a fuller study of the matter. In this mono-

9. Grote, *History of Greece*, 2:178.

10. Georg Busolt, *Griechische Geschichte bis zur Schlacht bei Chaeronea*, 2nd ed., 4 vols. (Gotha: Perthes, 1893), 1:506–07.

11. W. G. Forrest, *The Emergence of Greek Democracy 800–400 B.C.* (New York: McGraw-Hill, 1966), pp. 45–46.

12. Lillian Jeffery, *Archaic Greece* (New York: St. Martin's, 1976), pp. 39–40.

13. Andreev, "Könige," pp. 380–82.

graph I shall argue that the conventional picture is indeed incorrect: although there seem to have been some monarchies in Greece—specifically in Messenia, Arcadia, and other *ethnē*—during the ninth and eighth centuries, the evidence indicates that during this period most communities—and specifically those which in the Classical period we refer to as *poleis*—were ruled by small groups of hereditary leaders. The same had probably been true for the tenth century, but since the tenth century is so far removed from our literary sources, it will be safer to limit our generalizations to the Geometric period (900–720 B.C.).

The belief that through all or most of the Geometric period the Greeks were ruled by kings rests, so far as I can determine, on four very questionable pieces of evidence. First, and most influential, is the apparent ubiquity of kings in the *Iliad* and *Odyssey*. Second, authors such as Strabo and Pausanias have things to say about kings of various cities after the Return of the Heraclidae and the subsequent Neleid settlement of Ionia. Third, the chronographers give us Corinthian and Athenian kinglists which run to the middle of the eighth century. Fourth, in the Archaic period (720–500 B.C.) there were in a number of city-states officials who bore the title *basileus,* and it is assumed that this republican *basileia* in the Archaic period attests to the existence of a monarchy in the Geometric period.

Now the first of these bases—Homer's stories of heroic kings—must for several reasons be disallowed as evidence for the Geometric period. When the *Iliad* says that Agamemnon was king of Mycenae, or that Nestor was king of Pylos, a fundamentalist must take the statements at face value, and must proceed, on the basis of what Homer says about Agamemnon and Nestor, to sketch the features of monarchy during the Mycenaean Age, the Late Helladic III period. The fundamentalist approach is out of fashion, for the epigraphical and archaeological evidence makes it all too clear that in Mycenaean Greece there is no room for the kind of king that Homer describes. Accordingly, Homeric kingship is now commonly assigned to the Dark Age, where there is room for almost anything, since there is little archaeological and no epigraphical evidence around which one must maneuver. What archaeologists have found at Dark Age sites does not suggest the presence of kings—no palaces have been discovered, and, with an exception on Cyprus, no royal tombs—but it is true that the material record for most of the Dark Ages is still too limited to afford much of an argument on either side.[14]

But there is another reason for refusing to admit Agamemnon and Nestor to the Dark Age. If it were certain that the Homeric world once existed in mainstream Greece (Crete and the Peloponnese; the Isthmus, Attica, Euboea, and Boeotia; and eventually the coast of Asia Minor), then by eliminating the Bronze Age one would be left with the Dark Age as the only possible time in which the Homeric world, including kings such as Agamemnon and Nestor, could have existed. There is, however, no certainty that at any period the Homeric world existed in mainstream Greece. I have argued elsewhere that the Greeks' heroic traditions originated not in mainstream Greece—not, that is, in the Mycenaean south—but in the more primitive and bellicose Aeolic north, above all in Thessaly.[15] Most scholars are agreed that Homer was mistaken, and that

14. A. M. Snodgrass's inaugural lecture as Laurence Professor of Classical Archaeology at the University of Cambridge, *Archaeology and the Rise of the Greek State* (Cambridge: Cambridge Univ. Press, 1977), p. 9, suggests that on the question of the survival or disappearance of hereditary kingship "archaeology is unlikely to throw much light." Yet it is significant that in surveying (p. 16) the "rich graves" of the Geometric period, Snodgrass (correctly, I think) does not even raise the possibility that one or another might be royal. Andreev, "Könige," p. 379, n. 4, observes that "die einzige Königsbeisetzung während des ganzen Zeitraums vom 12. bis 8. Jh. v. u. Z. wurde vor relativ kurzer Zeit in der Nähe von Salamis auf Zypern entdeckt, aber das ist die Ausnahme, die eher die Regel bestätigt." On the tombs at Salamis and Kourion: Vassos Karageorghis, *Salamis in Cyprus* (London: Thames and Hudson, 1969), pp. 50–62; Wilson Strand, *Voices of Stone: The History of Ancient Cyprus* (Nicosia: Zavallis, 1974), p. 97.

15. R. Drews, "Argos and Argives in the *Iliad*," *CP* 74 (1979):111–35.

Agamemnon does not belong in thirteenth-century Mycenae. But we are not, therefore, obliged to relocate Agamemnon in the Argolid of the Dark Age, or to divide his traits between Late Helladic III Mycenae and Dark Age Argos. In whole or in part, Homer's Agamemnon may reflect traditions from outside mainstream Greece, traditions about Thessalian warlords being the most obvious possibility. That Homeric kingship reflects an institution of mainstream Greece during the Dark Age is nothing more than an assumption (and, I should say, an improbable assumption), urgently in need of some evidence on which to rest. Let us see what evidence there is for kingship in Greece during the Geometric period.

Ancient writers believed that kingship prevailed everywhere in heroic times and at the time of the Return of the Heraclidae and the migration of the Neleids; but it is worth noting that no ancient writer makes the generalization that kingship lasted until, in our terms, the eighth century. Polybius theorized that the cycle of constitutions begins with monarchy, which degenerates into tyranny and is then replaced by aristocracy.[16] In Rome, one supposes, this happened in the sixth century, but when it happened in Greece Polybius does not say. Nor do Aristotle and Plato provide any support for the belief that the Greeks were ruled by kings until the eighth century. According to Aristotle's *Politics*, kingship was not congenial to the Hellenic temper, and the only kinds of kingship that Aristotle recognized among the Greeks were the Spartan and the heroic, which existed "in the heroic times."[17] Although heroic times may be stretched a bit beyond the *nostoi* or even the Return of the Heraclidae, it is unlikely that under that term Aristotle could have included a period which was as close to his own day as it was to the Trojan War. Plato is even less forthcoming: in the *Republic* (544C) kingship is not listed among the four Hellenic types of government. As for Thucydides, only in a

---

16. Polybius 6.7–8.
17. Aristotle *Politics* 1285a–b. At *Pol.* 1252b Aristotle says that "initially" the *poleis* were ruled by kings, and that "even now" the *ethnē* are so ruled.

mistranslation does he bring kingship into, and even well beyond, Homer's day: after the Dorian migration, and after the
dispatch of colonies to east and west, Greece became more
powerful and wealthy, "the revenues of her cities increased,
and in most of them tyrannies were established; they had hitherto been ruled by hereditary kings, having fixed prerogatives."
So Jowett's translation of Thucydides 1.13. Jowett's "hitherto," alas, is the Greek πρότερον. Thucydides did not intend to
say that kingship lasted until the days of the first tyrants (thus
omitting aristocracy altogether).[18] What he meant to say is
that tyranny first appeared after the age of colonization: there
had been monarchs in the past, but they had been legitimate
kings and not tyrants. How long before the age of tyranny these
legitimate kings had ruled, Thucydides does not say, but the
sensible assumption is that he had in mind the heroic kings.
Thucydides, then, supplies no more evidence for kings in Geometric Greece than do Plato and Aristotle. Herodotus, who
ferreted out as many stories about post-heroic Greece as he
could find, seems to have heard no stories about Greek kings
after the sons of Codrus.

Nor do the poets of the Archaic period give any indication
that the land had until recently been ruled by kings. The Greek
kings alluded to in those fragments of lyric poetry that survive
all belong to the heroic period (Theopompus, the Spartan
basileus recalled by Tyrtaeus, is an exception; but Sparta, as
we shall see, presents a special case).[19] The epic poet from
Corinth, Eumelus, may possibly have referred to a king from
the post-heroic period: in the *Processional Hymn to Delian
Apollo,* composed by Eumelus for the Messenians when first
they sacrificed at Delos, there may have been a reference to a
reigning Messenian king, Phintas.[20] There is no indication, on

---

18. Andreev, "Könige," p. 382, also misunderstands the sentence and suggests that the only way out is to identify Thucydides' *basileia* as "eine Form
der Adelsherrschaft."

19. Tyrtaeus no. 4 (Diehl).

20. Pausanias 4.4.1: cf. Eumelus fr. 13 (Kinkel).

the other hand, that Eumelus' epic on Corinth mentioned any post-heroic Corinthian king.

Hesiod, whom we might date ca. 700 B.C., also said nothing about recent kings. He reports that his song had won a tripod at the funeral contests for Amphidamas of Chalcis, contests which the sons of that great-hearted man had celebrated.[21] Amphidamas is occasionally called a king in modern scholarship, but Hesiod does not call him that. Only in the *Contest of Homer and Hesiod,* written no earlier than ca. 400 B.C., do we learn, along with a host of other unlikely details about the contest, that Amphidamas was "king of Euboea" (line 315). Of course it is no surprise that Hesiod says nothing about post-heroic kings, since the subjects of the *Works and Days* and the *Theogony* provided little opportunity for allusions to persons or events after the heroic period. It is significant, however, that Hesiod explicitly discounts any continuity between the Race of Heroes and his own dreadful Iron Race. As he stated it in his myth, those heroes who did not perish at Thebes and Troy were transported to the Isles of the Blest, and Zeus then created the fifth and last race of mortals.[22] Unlike the Greeks of the Classical period, Hesiod apparently did not believe in Dark Age lines descended from Heracles, Neleus, or Agamemnon.

In summary, the Greeks themselves are not responsible for the doctrine that in the Greek states kingship lasted approximately until Homer's time, when there was a general shift from monarchy to aristocracy. Let us now turn from those authors who do not know about kingship in Geometric Greece to those texts which are used to prove its existence. We may begin with Ionia, and the traditions of the Neleid kings.

---

21. *Works and Days* 654–56. For King Amphidamas see, e.g., M. Cary, in *CAH* III (1929), 621; or, more recently, R. J. Hopper, *The Early Greeks* (London: Weidenfeld and Nicolson, 1976), p. 122. M. L. West, *Hesiod Theogony* (Oxford: Clarendon, 1966), pp. 43–44, is also inclined to see Amphidamas as "a Chalcidian king."

22. *Works and Days* 156–73.

CHAPTER II THE KINGS REPORTED IN GREEK TRADITION

THE EASTERN AEGEAN AND ASIA MINOR

IONIA

Homer and Hesiod say nothing about Codrid or Neleid kings in Ionia, but Homer was obviously familiar with stories about Neleus. In the *Iliad*, Neleus' garrulous son, Nestor, has something to say about his father, and the poet of the *Odyssey* helps to fill in the outline of the eighth-century story.[1] Neleus was the son of Poseidon and Tyro, daughter of Aeolus' great son, Salmoneus. Poseidon had lain in love with Tyro on the banks of the Enipeus River in Thessaly, for which occasion Poseidon had disguised himself as the river god. Grown to manhood, Neleus wandered from Thessaly to Pylos, where he became king and sired twelve sons, the most renowned of them being Nestor and Periclymenus. (Hesiodic poets said that when fighting, Periclymenus had the power to change his form to that of any creature he wished.)[2] It was Neleus' fate to offend Heracles, who thereupon attacked Pylos. Though sparing Neleus himself, Heracles disposed of Periclymenus (swatting him, a Hesiodic poet says, when Periclymenus took the form of a bee)[3] and slew all the other sons of Neleus save Nestor, the only one of the twelve to survive.

1. *Iliad* 11.670–97; *Odyssey* 11.235–59.
2. Hesiod fr. 33a (Merkelbach and West), from the *Aeolidae*. The fragment also names the twelve sons of Neleus and Chloris.
3. Hesiod fr. 33b (Merkelbach and West).

Most Ionians of the Archaic period believed that their ancestors had emigrated from Neleus' Pylos, and presumably they regarded their twelve cities as founded by offspring of Neleus' twelve sons. But Athens too, justifiably, claimed to be the Ionians' homeland, and writers identified an Athenian Neleus as the Ionian patriarch. For the Ionian nobles, however (especially in the Archaic period), the Neleus from whom they were sprung was surely the heroic son of Poseidon (the Athenian Alcmaeonids and Pisistratids also claimed descent from Pylian Neleus).[4] Mimnermus, writing ca. 600 B.C., stated that Colophon had been founded by "Pylian Andraemon,"[5] and some elegiac lines of Mimnermus leave Athens quite out of the picture:[6]

> When leaving the city of Neleian Pylos
> We came in ships to pleasant Asia,
> And sat us down at lovely Colophon. . . .

Athens as the point of departure appears first in the *Genealogies* that Pherecydes of Athens published soon after the Persian Wars. Here the Ionian *apoikia* is led by Androclus, identified as the founder of Ephesus and a legitimate son of Codrus, king of Athens.[7] Presumably Pherecydes gave currency to what became, for those concerned with such things, the standard genealogy of Codrus:[8]

Deucalion
Hellen
Aeolus

---

4. For the Alcmaeonid stemma see J. Toepffer s.v. Alkmaionidai, in *RE* I, 1556–58. The Pisistratids also claimed that originally they were Pylian Neleids (Herodotus 5.65.3).

5. Strabo 14.1.3.

6. Mimnermus no. 12 (Diehl).

7. Pherecydes (*F.Gr.Hist.* no. 3), fr. 155.

8. The genealogy is given by Hellanicus (*F.Gr.Hist.* no. 323a), fr. 23. Since Herodotus seems to have been familiar with the same genealogy (5.65.3), it must have had behind it the authority of a writer earlier than Hellanicus. Neither Melanthus nor Codrus appears in the Hesiodic corpus.

Salmoneus
   Tyro—Poseidon
      Neleus
      Periclymenus
      Boros
      Penthilus
      Andropompus
      Melanthus
      Codrus

Of special interest here are the last two entries. Melanthus, "the black" (who was the eponymous hero of Melainai, a deme in northwest Attica), was known in Athens, though hardly elsewhere, before Pherecydes' time. Melanthus was said to have defeated the Boeotian king, Xanthus ("the blond"), in single combat, thus preserving Melainai as an Athenian rather than a Boeotian community.[9] (In the fourth century Ephorus disclosed that the trick—*apatē*—by which Melanthus had won his victory was celebrated ever after in the festival of the Apaturia;[10] but this unflattering etymology had perhaps not yet been invented in Pherecydes' time.) This Athenian hero was presented by Pherecydes as a Neleid, who had fled from Pylos to Athens at the time that the Heraclidae returned to the Peloponnese and seized Messenia. Upon his arrival in Athens, Melanthus discovered the Athenians to be under attack by the Boeotians, with the Boeotian king challenging the Athenian king, Thymoetes, to single combat. The cowardly Thymoetes abdicated, and Melanthus took his place.

Codrus was also an Athenian hero of long standing. He is mentioned by Pherecydes, Herodotus, and Hellanicus, although the earliest extant account of his heroic death comes

---

9. Hellanicus (*F.Gr.Hist.* no. 323a), fr. 23; cf. Jacoby's commentary on this fragment, *A Commentary on the Ancient Historians of Athens* (Leiden: Brill, 1954), pp. 43–51.

10. Hellanicus may have given the etymology, for it appears in our source of Hellanicus fr. 23, a scholium on Plato's *Symposium*; elsewhere, however, it was attributed to Ephorus: see Ephorus (*F.Gr.Hist.* no. 70), fr. 22.

from the fourth century.[11] That he was well known in the fifth century can be deduced from his appearance on a red-figure cup of ca. 450 B.C. There he is shown bidding farewell to Aenetus, another Athenian hero.[12] Since Aenetus was the grandson of Xuthus, and since Aenetus' brothers had dealings with Erechtheus and Theseus, the artist perhaps imagined that Codrus too had lived before the Trojan War. Codrus' great achievement was his deliverance of Athens from an invasion by Peloponnesians. When and why the Peloponnesians had invaded was apparently a matter of debate; Herodotus at 5.76 states his opinion that the expedition in Codrus' time "could rightly be identified" with the Dorians' foundation of Megara. Whatever their objective, the Peloponnesians knew from an oracle that they could defeat the Athenians only if Codrus' life were spared. When Codrus learned of the oracle, he disguised himself as a beggar and walked out to the Peloponnesians' camp. While gathering firewood he provoked two of the Peloponnesians, and so was slain. When the invaders discovered the beggar's identity, they returned to the Peloponnese.

As son of Codrus, and leader of the Ionian migration, Pherecydes presented Androclus, who may have already enjoyed some reputation as the founder of Ephesus.[13] Herodotus (9.97), on the other hand, makes no mention of Androclus but does refer to "Neileus, the son of Codrus," identifying him as the founder of Miletus. In Hellanicus' account,[14] Neleus is the Codrid who leads the *apoikia* and founds all twelve Ionian cities (this extravagant claim did not catch on, and only the chronographer of the Parian Marble repeats it).[15] As time went by, the number of Codrus' sons multiplied; and after the list of

11. The story appears in Lycurgus, *In Leocratem* 84–87. It is clear that Pherecydes told the story much as it appears in Lycurgus' speech; see Pherecydes fr. 154.

12. J. D. Beazley, *Attic Red-Figure Vase-Painters*, 2nd ed., 3 vols. (Oxford: Clarendon, 1963), 2:1268, no. 1.

13. Pherecydes, fr. 155.

14. Hellanicus (*F.Gr.Hist.* no. 323a) fr. 23.

15. *Marmor Parium* = *F.Gr.Hist.* no. 239.

legitimate sons had been closed and canonized, Codrus' bastards were discovered to serve as founders of secondary cities. Such are the Ionian kings whom writers of the late Hellenistic and Roman periods know. Scholars who believe in these kings, or in the Neleid stemma, will not be disabused here of their faith. It is neither possible nor necessary to prove that the Codrid or Neleid kings of Ionia never existed. Our much more manageable task is to demonstrate that there is no evidence for kings in Geometric Ionia. This can be done most easily by establishing the dramatic dates of the kings: when were these kings, whether real or imaginary, said to have reigned? Quite clearly they were said to have reigned very soon after the Ionian cities were founded. J. M. Cook, who accepts the traditions about Ionian kingship, summarized their chronological span: "the later Greek traditions indicate that kingship was a universal institution in the Ionic cities in the generation or two after they were founded."[16] In the typical Ionian city Pausanias heard at least one story about the reign of the founder, and perhaps another about the founder's son and successor. That was usually the end of it, and a final story explained how and why the monarchy disappeared.[17]

Ephesus   Pherecydes tells us that Ephesus was founded by Androclus, son of Codrus. Later authors make Androclus both founder and king. Pausanias reports that Androclus led the Ephesians against Leogorus, king of Samos, and that the tomb of Androclus is on display at Ephesus, the tomb having upon it the figure of an armed man.[18] The fate of Androclus and his

---

16. J. M. Cook, "Early Greek Settlement in the Eastern Aegean and Asia Minor," *CAH²* II, 2, p. 804.

17. In his book on Peloponnesian Achaea (book 7) Pausanias digresses to describe the twelve Ionian cities which were regarded as peopled, in a roundabout way, with Achaean stock. That long digression provides us with most of our stories about Ionian kings. The stories of Pausanias and other late writers are conveniently assembled in G. L. Huxley's *The Early Ionians* (London: Faber and Faber, 1966), pp. 26–35.

18. Pausanias 7.2.8–9.

dynasty we learn from Stephanus of Byzantium:[19] while aiding the city of Priene, Androclus and many Ephesians were killed. The surviving Ephesians revolted against Androclus' sons (ἐστασίασαν κατὰ τῶν ᾽Ανδρόκλου παίδων), and as allies against them called in citizens of Teos and Mysian Karene. As a result, says Stephanus, two Ephesian tribes were named "Teians" and "Kareneians." Thus one story served to explain for the Ephesians the creation of two of their tribes and the end of the Androclid monarchy. We hear of no subsequent Ephesian kings.

Erythrae   The city of Erythrae was founded by Cnopus, bastard son of Codrus (Strabo 14.1.3). Here the monarchy seems to have perished with the oikist, for Cnopus is the only king of Erythrae mentioned in our sources. Athenaeus (259a) tells us that Cnopus was assassinated by some Erythraeans who set up their own oppressive oligarchic regime (Athenaeus is able to recite the regulations in minute detail). Finally, Hippotes, brother of Cnopus, freed the city. The story is introduced by Athenaeus as an explanation of how Cnopus' *basileia* came to an end.

Colophon   At Colophon, Pausanias (7.3.3–5) found three sons of Codrus: Andraemon (who in Mimnermus' poetry had been a Pylian), Damasichthon, and Promethus. What happened to Andraemon, Pausanias does not say. The other two brothers shared the kingship for a while; but then Promethus killed Damasichthon, and Promethus fled for his life to Naxos where he died. Damasichthon's sons, however, graciously permitted Promethus' body to be buried in Colophon, and his tomb (along with Andraemon's) could still be seen by the curious. That is all we hear about kings—or dyarchs—in Colophon. For those who doubt the existence of the Codrid troika, the oldest Colophonian state of which anything is known is the regime that Xenophanes recalled as existing before the Lydian wars with

---

19. Stephanus of Byzantium, s.v. Βέννα.

Colophon,[20] perhaps an aristocratic government with a citizen body of one thousand. On the basis of Xenophanes' poem or some other account, Aristotle (*Pol.* 1290b) classified the regime as oligarchic, even though the rich were also the many.

Phocaea   Like Colophon, Phocaea also had three kings, all at the same time. Pausanias (7.3.10) reports that when the Phocaeans arrived from Phocis (*sic*) they received land from the people of Cyme. "When the Ionians would not admit them to the Ionian confederacy until they accepted kings of the race of the Codridae, they accepted Deoetes, Periclus, and Abarnus from Erythrae and from Teos." Inscriptions from Phocaea reveal three tribal designations—Abarneus, Teuthadeus, and Perikleides—very much like the names of the Codrid triarchs,[21] and one may conclude that the Codrids began as eponymous heroes of the tribes. No other kings, whether single or in committee, are reported for Phocaea.

Teos   There is some unclarity about Teos. Pausanias (7.3.6) reports that Ionians were brought to the island of Teos by "a great-grandchild of Melanthus." This oikist has the wonderful name of Apoikos. Pausanias also says, in the same passage, that Attic settlers were brought by Damasus and Naoclus, both sons of Codrus, while Boeotians were led by Geres. What Pausanias seems to have in mind is a praesidium rather than a monarchy.

Myus   Plutarch (*de mul. virt.* 16) tells us about the small city of Myus. Some of the Ionians in Miletus, at odds with the sons of Neleus (στασιάσαντες πρὸς τοὺς Νείλεως παῖδας) went off to settle Myus. The Milesians made war upon them, though not without truces. During one festival-truce, Pieria, daughter of a

---

20. Xenophanes, no. 3 (Diehl).
21. *CIG* 3414, 3415 = *I G Rom*, 4.1325, 1326; Hesychius, s.v. ᾿Αβαρνεύς. In the manuscripts of Pausanias (7.3.10) the third king is Abartos. But Huxley, *Early Ionians*, p. 163, n. 77, argues persuasively that the proper reading must be Abarnos, for that name is attested not only at Phocaea, by Stephanus, but also at Phocaea's colony, Lampsacus, by Ephorus (*F.Gr.Hist.* no. 70). fr. 46.

prominent (*emphanes*) man, came from Myus to Miletus, and there Phrygius, who was the most powerful of the sons of Neleus, fell in love with her. Their romance brought the war to an end. The story does not envisage a monarchy at Myus (or at Miletus, for that matter), and in fact we hear nothing about kings of Myus. The founders were either the dissident Milesians, or Cydrelus, a bastard son of the indefatigable Codrus (Strabo 14.1.3).

Clazomenae, Lebedos, Priene Similarly, nobody is said to have been a king in Clazomenae, Lebedos, or Priene. There were confused and contradictory stories about the founders of these cities, but none of the founders is described as ruling his new city.

Miletus In addition to Neleus, the reputed founder of the city, four Milesian kings appear in stories, all written in the first century B.C. Two characters in one of the "erotic" tales of Parthenius[22] are kings of Miletus: Phobius and Phrygius. Phobius' wife fell in love with a young Halicarnassan named Antheus, and when the lad refused her overtures she slew herself; in grief Phobius turned his kingship over to Phrygius. The two kings, who are as real as the incident in which they are involved, should be sons of Neleus. We have just seen that Plutarch (*de mul. virt.* 16) knew a story about a Milesian Phrygius, whom he identified as the most powerful of Neleus' sons.

The other two Milesian kings, Amphitres (or Phitres) and Leodamas, appear in stories told by Conon the mythographer and Nicolaus of Damascus. Several scholars assign these kings to the late eighth century,[23] because in the stories Amphitres and Leodamas are the last of the Neleid kings, and traditionally the late eighth century is the appropriate time for dynasties to end. In fact, Conon and Nicolaus thought of their characters as

22. Parthenius, *Erot.* 14.
23. Huxley, *Early Ionians*, p. 50; Thomas, "From Wanax to Basileus," p. 187; for Jeffery, *Archaic Greece*, p. 210, "all this must have happened before the end of the seventh century, and may have begun at its start."

acting at the dawn of Miletus' existence. In Conon's story,[24] Leodamas and Phitres, both of the royal *genos*, are rival candidates for the throne, and an oracle commands that the throne be awarded to whichever of the two confers the greatest boon on the city. Phitres goes to war with Melos but accomplishes nothing. Leodamas defeats Euboean Carystus, and in his plunder brings back a woman and her young son. The boy becomes the ward of Branchus, who has just founded his oracle at Branchidae. Branchus gives to the boy the task of conveying oracular announcements to those making inquiry, and the boy is therefore named "Euangelus." From him are descended the Euangelidae, who have ever after remained in charge of the oracle.

Nicolaus' story opens with Amphitres slaying Leodamas and taking the throne by force.[25] The partisans of Leodamas flee the city and while they are in exile two Phrygian youths come to them bearing the sacred cult objects of the Cabiri. With the aid of the youths and their objects, the exiles defeat Amphitres. The Milesian *demos* establishes the cult of the Cabiri and then elects, in place of a king, an *aisymnētēs*, Epimenes by name. Instructed by the *demos*, Epimenes sets a bounty of silver for anyone who can slay the sons of Amphitres. The property that had belonged to Amphitres is confiscated, three of his faction are killed, and the remainder flee the city. "Thus," concludes Nicolaus, "were the Neleids brought to an end."

Gustave Glotz observed long ago that Nicolaus' story seems to have arisen from an imaginative reading of an inscription from the middle of the fifth century.[26] The inscription records

24. Conon (*F. Gr. Hist.* no. 26), fr. 1. sect. 44.
25. Nicolaus (*F.Gr.Hist.* no. 90), fr. 52 and 53.
26. For Glotz's analysis see *CRAcad. Inscr.* (1906), pp. 511–29. For the inscription see R. Meiggs and D. Lewis, *A Selection of Greek Historical Inscriptions* (Oxford: Clarendon, 1969), no. 43. The names of the banished were Alcimus and Cresphontes. According to a scholiast at *Iliad* 11.692, Alcimus was one of the twelve sons of Neleus (though he does not appear on the Hesiodic list; see above, n. 2). Cresphontes is familiar as the original Heraclid king of Messenia.

a decree banishing certain Neleids from Miletus, and ordering the *epimenios* (a monthly official) to pay a bounty, from the confiscated property of the confederates, for their lives. The banishment was almost certainly a result of the abortive Milesian revolt against Athens in 446–43 B.C.[27] But the odd Milesian who amused himself by reading ancient inscriptions might not have been able to discover that. What we have of the decree comes from the base of a stele, and it is possible that the base had already been separated from its stele when Nicolaus' source chanced upon it.

In whatever manner these stories may have originated, when did Conon and Nicolaus suppose that Leodamas and Amphitres reigned? The evidence is supplied by the synchronisms in the stories. Undoubtedly the Milesians thought that their cult of the Cabiri was very old, though we have no information about their opinion on this matter. We do, however, know some opinions about the age of the oracle at Branchidae. One view, transmitted by John Tzetzes, held that the oracle was even older than Miletus, for Neleus consulted the oracle before founding the city.[28] For our purposes, it is an ususual piece of luck that Conon, the very mythographer who tells the story of Leodamas, Branchus, and Euangelus, also tells a story about the birth of Branchus.[29] Smikros of Delphi, on orders of Apollo, migrated to Miletus and there married a Milesian girl. After she had become pregnant she dreamt that she had been penetrated by the sun. She gave birth to a boy of exceptional appearance, and the boy, Branchus, grew up to become Apollo's lover (Apollo's kiss gave him his oracular powers). It is doubtful that Conon believed much or anything of his story; the point is that his dramatic date for Leodamas and Amphitres is the age when Branchus and Apollo were lovers. That age was not the late eighth century. Leodamas and Amphitres belong

27. J. P. Barron, "Milesian Politics and Athenian Propaganda," *JHS* 82 (1962):1–6.

28. F. Cauer, s.v. Branchidai, *RE* III, 809.

29. Conon (*F.Gr.Hist.* no. 26), fr. 1, sect. 33.

not to history but to myth. The Hellenistic Milesians assumed that their ancestors had begun electing republican magistrates at about the time that the cult of the Cabiri and the oracle at Branchidae were established. As in the other Ionian cities, there is no evidence for, and no tradition about, Milesian kings of the Geometric period.

Chios   As kings of Chios we find not only several shadowy figures, but also the most familiar of all Dark Age kings, Hector of Chios. Hector too had been confined to the shadows until H. T. Wade-Gery spotlighted him in *The Poet of the Iliad.* Locating Hector ca. 800 B.C., Wade-Gery proposed that this king of Chios provided the name, at least, for Homer's Hector.[30] Since Wade-Gery's attention to him, Hector has frequently been cited as an example of the kings of Geometric Greece. Let us have a closer look at him and the other reputed kings of Chios.

Our knowledge of the Chian kings comes from Pausanias 7.4.8 (King Hector appears nowhere else in extant classical literature). In this instance, Pausanias found his information not in Hellenistic or Roman sources but in *The Foundation of Chios,* an early prose work written in the Periclean Age by Ion of Chios. Ion was famous as a poet, especially as a tragedian, and the titles which have come down to us center mostly on Heracles and the Trojan cycle. Here, then, is the fragment from Pausanias, given in the course of the Periegete's long digression on the twelve cities of Ionia:

Ion the tragic poet says in his history that Poseidon came to the island when it was uninhabited; that there he had intercourse with a nymph, and that when she was in her pains there was a fall of snow [*chion*], and that accordingly Poseidon called his son Chios. Ion also says that Poseidon had intercourse with another nymph, by whom he had Agelus and Melas; that in course of time Oenopion too sailed with a fleet from Crete to Chios, accompanied by his sons Talus, Euanthes, Melas, Salagus and Athamas. Carians too came to the island, in the

30. H. T. Wade-Gery, *The Poet of the Iliad* (Cambridge: Cambridge Univ. Press, 1952), pp. 6–8.

reign of Oenopion, and Abantes from Euboea. Oenopion and his sons were succeeded by Amphiclus, who because of an oracle from Delphi came from Histiaea in Euboea. Three generations from Amphiclus, Hector, who also had made himself king, made war on those Abantes and Carians who lived in the island, slew some in battle, and forced others to surrender and depart. When the Chians were rid of war, it occurred to Hector that they ought to unite with the Ionians in sacrificing at Panionium. It is said that the Ionian confederacy gave him a tripod as a prize for valour. Such was the account of the Chians that I found given by Ion. However, he gives no reason why the Chians are classed with the Ionians.

When he summarized this charming story, Wade-Gery transmogrified it into history. In place of the ancient title, *The Foundation of Chios,* Wade-Gery renames the work *The Hellenic Conquest,* suggesting that it was a grim military history. In Wade-Gery's summary there is nothing about Poseidon and his nymphs and the snow. Nor is there anything about Oenopion and his five sons. Instead, Ion is represented as saying only that "at first a mixed population had the island." Although even the infant Chios, to say nothing of Oenopion and his sons, have good Greek names, Wade-Gery concluded that Ion's Amphiclus was "no doubt the first king of Greek Chios, the leader of the systematic Hellenic Conquest: and we should probably therefore put him about 900 B.C. or a little earlier: not much earlier." With Amphiclus nicely dated it is easy enough to find a date for Hector. "Hektor, the great-grandson, should be dated about a century later than Amphiklos: 800 B.C. or a little earlier or later."

There are, however, no grounds for dating Amphiclus to 900 B.C. That date was merely Wade-Gery's date, archaeologically based, for the Ionian migration. One might today suggest that Amphiclus be moved back to 1000 B.C., and Hector to 900 B.C., since the archaeological date for the migration is now a century earlier than it was when Wade-Gery was writing.[31] But

---

31. G. M. Hanfmann, *AJA* 64 (1960):199; J. M. Cook, "Early Greek Settlement," p. 785.

that does not meet the real objection: *any* date transfers Amphiclus from the world of myth to pedestrian history. As an analogous operation, one could as justifiably date Romulus to the late seventh century, on the basis of the archaeological evidence for the foundation of Rome.

It happens that another fragment of Ion's writings, this one not cited by Wade-Gery, shows us what Ion thought about Oenopion's, and so about Amphiclus' era. In a pentameter quoted by Plutarch (*Theseus* 20.2) Ion says that Oenopion was the son of Theseus and Ariadne. Although Ion hardly constructed a chronology for these legendary events, his story placed Amphiclus in the third generation after Theseus, and Hector in the third generation after that. Let us compare that sequence with the sequence of Athenian kings given by the ancient chronographers:[32]

Ion	*Chronographers*
Theseus	Theseus
Oenopion	Menestheus
	Demophon (Theseus' son)
Oenopion's sons	Oxuntes
Amphiclus	Aphidas
First generation	Thymoetes
	Melanthus
Second generation	Codrus
Hector	Codrus' sons

As Felix Jacoby pointed out in 1947, in an article which appeared too late for Wade-Gery's consideration in *The Poet of the Iliad*, Ion was paying Athens a special tribute when he made Oenopion the son of Theseus.[33] Hitherto Oenopion had

---

32. Eusebius *Chron.* 1, cols. 181–86 (Schoene), gives the list as found in the *Chronica* of Castor of Rhodes. The main lines of the list were worked out by Hellanicus of Lesbos; see below, pp. 89–90.

33. Felix Jacoby, "Some Remarks on Ion of Chios," *CQ* 41 (1947):1–17.

been thought of as a son of Dionysus. By making him a son of Theseus, Ion affiliated Chios to Athens in remotest times.[34] That Ion told of no son of Codrus leading Ionians to Chios, an omission which puzzled Pausanias, is thus no surprise at all: the royal Athenian line had branched to Chios long before the other Ionian cities were founded.

So much can be said with certainty about Ion's story. Perhaps we may also infer the intent of his sentences about Hector. If there were traditions that Chios had once been inhabited by Abantes and Carians, there would also be a story explaining how this barbarian stock had been eradicated, leaving the island with a pure Hellenic population. Ion credited the debarbarization to a grandson of Amphiclus, "who also had made himself king." Since Ion's Hector is contemporary with the sons of Codrus, perhaps Ion imagined that Hector attached Chios to the Ionian League as soon as the Codrids had founded the other eleven cities.

In short, while we cannot prove that Oenopion, Amphiclus, and Hector never reigned in Chios, we must not transfer them from myth to history. Ion thought of them as living in the mythical past, and we cannot make Geometric kings of them.

Moving on from the mythical figures, we come to consider Hippoclus, the only other figure who might have been a king of Chios. Hippoclus was not mentioned by Ion, and clearly was not regarded as one of Chios' heroic kings. He appears once, in one of Plutarch's anecdotes (*de mul. virt. 3*). We shall need to glance at the story in order to make a balanced judgment about Hippoclus:

The Chians settled Leuconia for some such reason as this: one of those who were considered notables [*gnorimoi*] on Chios was getting married. As the bride was being brought in a chariot, the *basileus* Hippoclus, who was a close friend of the groom and who was there in attendance along with the rest, in the general drunkenness and fri-

---

34. The Oenopes, whose eponymous Oenopion was, were one of the Ionian tribes. See Carl Roebuck, "Tribal Organization in Ionia," *TAPA* 92 (1961):497.

volity leaped up onto the chariot; he meant to do nothing outrageous, but was merely following the common custom of tomfoolery. But the friends of the groom killed him.

An oracle, continues Plutarch, ordered that Hippoclus' slayers themselves be slain. But when everybody who was in any way involved insisted on sharing the guilt, the Chians sent the whole lot off to Leuconia (probably on the Anatolian mainland opposite the city of Chios), a place which the Coroneans, with assistance from Erythrae, had earlier appropriated.[35] Later, during a war between Erythrae and Chios, the Erythraeans forced the Chians to evacuate the city (though with their honor saved, thanks to the spirit of the Chians' womenfolk).

Let us grant that this is not a late novella, but a historical tradition, preserved somehow until Plutarch's time. When would the death of Hippoclus have occurred? Herodotus (1.18) speaks of "the Chians' war against the Erythraeans" as having occurred before the Lydian war with Thrasybulus of Miletus, but not so long before it that the Chians had forgotten the help which the Milesians had given them against Erythrae. A reasonable guess would place the Erythraean war with Chios in the second half of the seventh century, and we may therefore suppose that Chios had colonized Leuconia in the first half of the seventh century.

Was Chios ruled by a king in the early seventh century? Other than his title,[36] there is nothing in the anecdote to indicate that Hippoclus was a king. And several items in the anecdote suggest rather strongly an aristocratic regime: Hippoclus' milieu of prominent friends; the nature of his escapade; the lack of hesitation in dispatching him when he misbehaved; the absence of a successor to the throne; and even Hippoclus' name. Now although we do not know that the Chians ever had a king (and if they resembled the other Ionians they did not), there is no doubt whatever that in Archaic Chios there were

35. In the Loeb edition of F. C. Babbitt, the role of the Coroneans is mistranslated.
36. ὁ βασιλεὺς Ἵπποκλος.

basileis. The well known "Constitution of Chios,"[37] found on an inscription dating from ca. 575 B.C., shows that at the time the island was a republic, not a monarchy: there is a "popular council" (*dēmosiē bolē;* the differentiating adjective implies that there may also have been an aristocratic council)[38] which meets monthly, there are *dēmarchoi,* and there are *basileis.* We must pause here to deal with a lexical difficulty. Most of us would prefer, when discussing the Chian *dēmarchoi,* to transliterate the Greek term, or to Anglicize it as "demarchs," rather than to translate it as "popular leaders." A translation would inevitably distort the meaning of the term. Similarly, when dealing with Athenian *archontes* and Roman *consules,* we do not translate them, but Anglicize them as "archons" and "consuls." The word *basileus,* on the other hand, has unfortunately been regarded as covering precisely the same semantic field as the English word "king." One therefore has felt no more reluctance to translate *basileus* as "king" than to translate *lithos* as "stone." One of the purposes of this monograph is to discover what the word *basileus* did in fact mean in Archaic Greece. In later times it most often meant king, and there is usually little risk in so translating it when it appears in Strabo or Pausanias. In Chios, ca. 575 B.C., it obviously could mean something else, and we shall therefore do the word least violence if we render it as a technical term.

Returning to our Chian *basileis,* we note that there was a college of them, as of the *dēmarchoi* (a later inscription shows that a single *basileus,* identified as "the *basileus*" held a non-collegial magistracy).[39] The Chian law of 575 B.C. is so badly

---

37. Ulrich von Wilamowitz-Moellendorff, *Nordionische Steine* (Abhandlungen der Königlich preussischen Akademie der Wissenschaften: Philosophisch-historische Klasse, 1909), p. 64. Meiggs and Lewis, *Greek Historical Inscriptions,* no. 8.

38. L. H. Jeffery, "The Courts of Justice in Archaic Chios," *ABSA* 51 (1956): p. 166.

39. A fifth-century inscription, no. 688 in E. Schwyzer's *Dialectorum Graecarum exempla epigraphica potiora* (Leipzig, 1923) refers to a singular *basileus;* no. 693 in the same collection refers to the college. See Jeffery, "Courts," p. 165.

preserved that it is not clear whether it stipulates a fine in case the *basileis* and *dēmarchoi* are bribed (which would probably indicate a judicial function), or whether it stipulates how those officials are to administer a cult.[40] Nor do we know whether the Chian *basileis* had an annual term, as did the *basileus* in Archaic Athens, or whether they were in office for a longer period. At any rate, the existence of republican *basileis* in Archaic Chios is certain. If someone named Hippoclus did in fact once hold the title *basileus* in Chios, he was a republican magistrate.

Samos Samos is the twelfth and last Ionian state in our review. Asius, a Samian poet of the Archaic period, wrote that Astypalaea, daughter of Phoenix, had by Poseidon a son whom she named Ancaeus, and he reigned over the Leleges in Samos.[41] Later writers told how the first Greeks were led to Samos by Procles of Epidaurus, descended from Xuthus and Ion. After Procles' death, his son Leogorus ruled, but in his time Androclus brought colonists from Attica to Ephesus, and for a short time expelled Leogorus and his people from Samos.[42]

These *Urgestalten*, ironically, are more familiar to our late writers than were some of the historical tyrants who ruled Samos in the late seventh and sixth centuries. In the spectrum of time and reality that separates Leogorus from the tyrant Demoteles (ca. 600 B.C.),[43] there is only one figure whom we must consider, and he has impeccable credentials as a real person. Herodotus, after describing the misfortunes which a group of Samians suffered at the hands of the Aeginetans, in the aftermath of the attack on Samos by Sparta (ca. 525 B.C.), explained why the Aeginetans acted so churlishly:

40. J. H. Oliver, "Text of the So-called Constitution of Chios from the First Half of the Sixth Century B.C.," *AJP* 80 (1959):296–301, argues in favor of the second alternative; Jeffery, "Courts," in favor of the first.

41. Asius fr. 7 (Kinkel) = Pausanias 7.4.1.

42. Pausanias 7.4.2; cf. Strabo 14.1.3.

43. J. P. Barron, "The Sixth-Century Tyranny at Samos," *CQ* 14 (1964):211.

The Aeginetans did these things because they had a grudge against the Samians. Earlier Samians, at the time that Amphicrates was the *basileus* in Samos (ἐπ᾽ Ἀμφικράτεος βασιλεύοντος ἐν Σάμῳ), made an expedition against Aegina and did the Aeginetans much harm, and also suffered some harm from them. This, then, was the reason. [3.59.4]

While the anecdote about Hippoclus, *basileus* in Chios, might be apocryphal, there is no reason to doubt that Amphicrates was once *basileus* in Samos. He does not figure in an aetiological yarn or *mythos*, but in a prosaic tradition. Nor should it be argued that he was a tyrant. Although there is a persistent belief that Herodotus used the words *basileus* and *tyrannos* interchangeably, a careful review shows that although he may have called some odious kings tyrants, he did not refer to a tyrant as a *basileus*.[44]

When the original war between Samos and Aegina occurred, and so when Amphicrates lived, cannot be determined; but the first half of the sixth century is the best possibility. The war must have occurred at least a generation before the Aeginetans' reprisal ca. 525 B.C., for Herodotus says that earlier Samians had conducted the war. Aegina was associated with Samos and ten other Anatolian Greek states in the building of temples at Naucratis under the Egyptian King Amasis (569–26 B.C.), although the association was not necessarily congenial: whereas nine states collaborated in building one temple, the Aeginetans, Samians, and Milesians built each their own temples, to Zeus, Hera, and Apollo respectively.[45] Perhaps com-

44. Arthur Ferrill, "Herodotus on Tyranny," *Historia* 27 (1978):391, finds that of the 860 instances of the words *basileus* and *basileia* in Herodotus' work, only one may be Herodotus' own reference to a tyrant (5.35.1: Aristagoras "thought that he would be stripped of the *basileia* of Miletus"). In all other instances of confusion, it is a subject or a flatterer who addresses a tyrant as *basileus*. Ferrill also concludes that a true king who governs his subjects reasonably rather than despotically is never called a *tyrannos* by Herodotus. One apparent exception is 8.137.1, where Herodotus refers to the Macedonian royal house as a *tyrannis*.

45. Herodotus 2.178.

petition at Naucratis reflected or touched off a war between Aegina and Samos. In very early times feelings were said to have been friendly, for there was a tradition that the original wooden statue of Hera in the Samian Heraeum was carved by an Aeginetan.[46]

Several observations can be made about Amphicrates' position. Whereas in Archaic Chios a college of *basileis* is attested, the reference to Amphicrates shows that he did not have a colleague. It is also significant that the only purpose he serves in the Herodotean account is to date the war. Though none of us knows when Amphicrates was *basileus,* Herodotus' contemporaries must have known, or at least must have been able to find out, from someone more knowledgeable about Samos' past. The chronological indices which came down from the Archaic to the Classical period were furnished not by annual magistrates but by figures who were in the limelight for extended periods. (Late in the fifth century various states began using the name of an annual magistrate as a dating device, and it was then that official lists of eponymous magistrates were drawn up, the lists of Athenian archons being the most important.) The tyrants and the Spartan *basileis* served this purpose well.[47] That Amphicrates did the same suggests that he was

46. Aethlios of Samos (*F.Gr.Hist.* no. 536), in the fifth book of his *Annals of Samos,* said (fr. 3) that at one time the *agalma* of Samian Hera was a plank or slab, and that when Procles was ruler the thing was given human shape. Pausanias 7.4.4 came to the conclusion that the sanctuary was one of the oldest anywhere, basing his conclusion on the statue: "for it is the work of an Aeginetan, Smilis, the son of Eucleides. This Smilis was a contemporary of Daedalus. . . ." A papyrus commentary on Callimachus states that before the time of King Procles there was not a proper statue of Hera at Samos, only an unworked block of wood brought from Argos, and that the wood from which the statue was made (undoubtedly the same Argive block) could still be seen at the Samian Heraeum. For the papyrus see Jacoby's commentary, *F.Gr.Hist.* no. 536, n. 5.

47. Alden Mosshammer, *The Chronicle of Eusebius and Greek Chronographic Tradition* (Lewisburg, Pa.: Bucknell Univ. Press, 1979), p. 90: "The few events of early Spartan history that carry chronological references in the sources are dated by Olympiads or king years, never eponymous ephors." The lists published late in the fifth century made possible the use of archon years or

basileus for a much longer time than one year. It therefore appears that at a time when Archaic Samos was not under a tyrant (though perhaps not after the long tyranny of Polycrates), the chief officer in the state was a *basileus* who held his position for an extended tenure, perhaps even for life. We do not, as it happens, have any information about Samian magistracies before the Persian Wars.[48] A tradition transmitted by Plutarch indicates that the oligarchy of the *geomoroi* was in power until some time after the Samians founded Perinthus[49] (traditionally in 602 B.C.), and it is therefore possible that the Samian *basileus* originally functioned within that oligarchic regime. We shall return to that possibility in the closing chapter.

In leaving Samos let us observe that the Samian kings about whom stories were told were the oikist and the oikist's son. There is no evidence for Samian kings in the Geometric period. And there apparently was a Samian *basileus* in the Archaic period.

AEOLIS

Pausanias' long excursus on the twelve Ionian cities gives us at least a few of the stories which later generations told about the early history of these states. We have nothing comparable for most of the Aeolian states of the northeast Aegean. There are

---

ephor years in written histories, beginning with Hellanicus' *Atthis*. The oral tradition tapped by Herodotus dated events by kings and tyrants. On the general question of eponymous magistrates see Mosshammer, *Chronicle*, pp. 88–91.

48. *Prytaneis* and *demiorgoi* are attested for the fourth century and the Hellenistic period, and it is likely that those magistracies existed already in the fifth century. In some years there was one *demiorgos* in office, in other years there were two; in the third century the *demiorgoi* were eponymous. See Christian Habicht, "Samische Volksbeschlüsse der hellenistischen Zeit," *MDAI* (1957):253, nn. 133 and 134. Inscription no. 4 in Habicht's collection, to be dated not long after 321 B.C., "enthält die älteste Erwähnung der Prytanen, die hier, wie später oft, als Antragsteller erscheinen."

49. Plutarch *Quaest. Graecae* 57 (303–04). At Samos the *geomoroi* seem to have constituted an oligarchy; see Thucydides 8.21 for the conflict between the Samian *demos* and the *geomoroi* in 412 B.C.

only two cities, Mytilene and Cyme, for which we have
enough information to permit a conjecture about their early
regimes, and a third, Smyrna, about which one can state only
an *argumentum ex silentio.*

Smyrna   The town of "Old Smyrna," at which considerable
archaeological work has been done but not published, is perhaps best known today from R. V. Nicholls's drawings[50] of
what the town may have looked like ca. 900 B.C. It does not, I
am happy to note, look like a town with a king. Nor does
Herodotus' account (1.50) of how the Ionians took the city
from the Aeolians suggest that in the fifth century there were
traditions about early Smyrnaean kings. Nowhere, in fact, do
we find stories about Aeolian or Ionian kings at Smyrna.

Mytilene   In seventh-century Lesbos the nobility of several
towns, including Mytilene, were known as the Penthilidae.
They were not remembered fondly, as an anecdote in Aristotle's *Politics* (1311b) shows: a Mytilenian named Megacles,
together with his friends, rose up against and slew the Penthilidae who had gone about striking the Mytilenians with clubs.
At the end of the seventh century the Penthilidae had been
reduced to sharing power with other aristocrats, at least in
Mytilene. For, in the aristocratic vendettas of Alcaeus' day the
Penthilidae were only a part of the faction opposed by Alcaeus
and his brothers.[51]

According to Stephanus of Byzantium, there was a polis on
Lesbos named Penthile.[52] If such a town existed in the Geo-

50. For the drawings see fig. 2 in *CAH*[2] II, 2, p. 798. Forrest, *Emergence of
Greek Democracy*, p. 76. The drawings first appeared in *ABSA* 53–54
(1958–59) p. 51. The essential article is J. M. Cook's "Old Smyrna,
1948–1951," pp. 1–34 in the same volume.

51. Pittacus married a Penthilid, to Alcaeus' chagrin. See Alcaeus nos. 70,
75, and 302 (ed. Lobel and Page), and the comments of D. L. Page, *Sappho and
Alcaeus* (Oxford: Oxford Univ. Press, 1955), p. 235. Although still prestigious,
the Penthilidae of Alcaeus' day seem to have been politically feeble.

52. Stephanus of Byzantium, s.v. Πενθίλη: "A polis of Lesbos. The citizens
are called *Penthileis.* Named after Penthilus." Scholar Höfer, in Roscher *Lex.*
III, 1943, s.v. Penthilus, proposed that Stephanus' Penthile "lebt in dem
heutigen Ortsnamen Πεντσίλη noch fort."

metric period, the Penthilidae will have gotten their name from it. They, of course, claimed an eponymous hero as their ancestor, Penthilus (whom Stephanus, predictably again, also regarded as the source of the town's name). They identified Penthilus as a grandson of Agamemnon and a son of Orestes, and said that he had led a great force from the Peloponnese to Lesbos. Some claimed that Penthilus himself had died en route, and that Archelaus had brought the Aeolians to their new home. Others said that Penthilus himself had seized the whole island.[53]

The story that Penthilus had once ruled all Lesbos is almost, but not quite, the only evidence that Mytilene was ever ruled by kings. "Ein weiteres Beweis, dass Mytilene ursprünglich eine Königsherrschaft war, ist das spätere Kollegium der βασίληες."[54] This argument too, as we shall see in chapter three, has no validity. There is no reason to suppose that during the Geometric period there was a monarchy in Mytilene.

The closest analogy to the Penthilidae of Lesbos is provided by the Aeolian homeland, Thessaly. When first we glimpse historical Thessaly, at the end of the sixth century, single aristocratic families (who trace their ancestry to heroes) control fairly wide areas: the Aleuadae ruled Larissa and neighboring towns, the largest town (it was hardly a city) in the land ruled by the Scopadae was Crannon, and the Echecratidae controlled

53. Strabo 13.1.3; Pausanias 3.2.1. Penthilus was never more than an obscure genealogical contrivance. The Archelaus whom Strabo identifies as Penthilus' son may at one time have been the founding hero of Mytilene. Plutarch (*Sept. sap. convivium* 20 = 163B) puts into the mouth of Pittacus a story that the colonizers of Lesbos were led by seven *basileis* and *archagetai*, whose *hēgemōn* was Echelaus.

54. R. Herbst, s.v. Mytilene, *RE* XVI, 1420–21. The college of *basileis* may have been as old as the city-state of Mytilene. According to Theophrastus (Stobaeus *Flor.* 44.22) a law of Pittacus ordered that property transactions should be concluded "in the presence of the *basileis* and the *prytanis.*" For the inscriptional evidence on the college of *basileis* and the single *prytanis* in Classical and Hellenistic Mytilene see Georg Busolt, *Griechische Staatskunde* 1 (Munich: Beck, 1920), p. 351, n. 2.

Pharsalus and a few minor towns.[55] This kind of primitive regime was looked upon by Greeks of the city-states not as a *politeia*, but as a *dynasteia*.[56] The Penthilidae seem to have been enjoying such a *dynasteia* over most of Lesbos when Megacles opposed them in seventh-century Mytilene. And the story that Penthilus was a son of Orestes shows that the people of Lesbos could not remember a time when the Penthilidae had not been in control.

Cyme   Aeolian Cyme presents more difficulty. Another figure who is conspicuous in Wade-Gery's *The Poet of the Iliad* was "King Agamemnon of Kyme whose daughter married Midas of Phrygia. That should be about 700 B.C. We owe King Agamemnon's name to Aristotle and probably to Ephoros."[57] Although Wade-Gery's reckoning would put Agamemnon outside the Geometric period, one could hardly accept Agamemnon as king without admitting that there was a royal line at Cyme through the eighth century. Agamemnon's credentials must therefore be inspected.

First of all, we do not owe his name to Aristotle. The pertinent Aristotelian fragment (fr. 611, no. 37, Rose) reads as follows:

They say that Hermodice, the wife of Midas, king of the Phrygians, was remarkably beautiful, but was also wise and skillful, and was the first to coin money for the Cymaeans.

That is all that Aristotle says on the matter: nothing on the name of Hermodice's father, or his occupation. For the name Agamemnon the sole witness is Julius Pollux (*Onomasticon* 9.83). Pollux observed that there was no agreement about the inventor of coinage,

---

55. H. D. Westlake, *Thessaly in the Fourth Century B.C.* (London: Methuen, 1935), p. 30.

56. At 4.78.3 Thucydides contrasted the Thessalian *dynasteia* with *isonomia*. The Theban orator at Thuc. 3.62.3 contrasts the old Theban *dynasteia* with both an *oligarchia isonomos* and a *demokratia*.

57. Wade-Gery, *Poet of the Iliad*, p. 7.

whether Pheidon the Argive was the first to strike coins, or Demodice, the Cymaean who lived with Midas the Phrygian—she was the
child of Agamemnon, *basileus* of the Cymaeans (παῖς δ' ἦν
'Αγαμέμνονος Κυμαίων βασιλέως), or Erichthonius and Lycus at Athens, or the Lydians, as Xenophanes says.[58]

Also pertinent to Agamemnon is a passage in the *Herodotean Life of Homer*. Wade-Gery cited the passage in support of
Agamemnon's historicity and as evidence that Midas' "parents-in-law from Kyme (that is, Agamemnon and his queen)
seem to have survived him."[59] (The passage also, incidentally,
supplies "evidence," for those who care to use it, that Homer
began his career after Midas' death.) At any rate, the wretched
biographer's tale begins with the blind Melesigenes—for that
was Homer's real name—in severe straits and deciding to seek
his fortune at Cyme. There he composed the epitaph (which
the biographer gives in full) which stands on the tomb of Midas
at Gordium. Melesigenes composed the epitaph at the request
of Midas' parents-in-law.

Thus far the story might strengthen one's belief in King
Agamemnon of Cyme, even though it does not mention him
by name. What follows, however, shows that the biographer
did not think of Homer's Cyme as a monarchy. The story goes
on to say that after composing Midas' epitaph, Melesigenes
began reciting his poetry in the lounge where the old men of
the city loitered. They were impressed, and Melesigenes promised them that if he were given a public endowment he would
make the city famous. His admirers urged him to take his
request to the *boulē*, and in the *boulē* various councillors
spoke for and against his request. One councillor in particular

58. The text of Pollux is corrupt precisely at the point that interests us. The
manuscript reading is utterly unintelligible: εἴτε δημοτικῇ ἡ κυβαίᾳ συνοικήσασα μηδὲ τῷ Φρυγὶ παῖς δ' ἦν 'Αγαμέμνονος κυβαίων βασιλεύς. Joachim
Kühn emended the text in his edition of 1696, and his emendation has been
accepted ever since. The text in E. Bethe's 1931 Teubner edition now reads:
εἴτε Δημοδίκη ἡ Κυμαία συνοικήσασα Μίδᾳ τῷ Φρυγί—παῖς δ' ἦν 'Αγαμέμνονος
Κυμαίων βασιλέως.

59. Wade-Gery, *Poet of the Iliad*, p. 65, n. 21.

urged that if Cyme gave support to every *homeros* (among the Cymaeans a *homeros* was a blind man) who asked for it, the city would soon be overrun with blind men. Melesigenes' request was turned down, but after that day he was called "Homeros."[60]

What does one make of all this? Surely in the late Classical and Hellenistic periods there was a story about a Cymaean woman, called either Hermodice or Demodice, who was both Midas' wife and the introducer of coinage into Cyme. That Midas had died almost a century before coinage was introduced was a fact that did not trouble the inventor of the story. It is difficult to imagine that a story which synchronized King Midas, a bronze statue, coinage, and perhaps even Homer, could have come into being before the fourth century.[61] And the standard version of the story does not seem to have made the Cymaean girl a daughter of the Cymaean king. That circumstance is not mentioned by Aristotle and is flatly incompatible with the anecdote in the *Herodotean Life of Homer*. The biographer's story will not, of course, be used by the prudent as evidence that in Homer's day Cyme was governed by a *boulē*. But it does make unlikely the existence of popular traditions about a king in Homeric Cyme.

There were *basileis* in Archaic Cyme, but they were not kings. We shall see that for Hesiod, whose father came from Cyme, *basileus* did not mean "king." More to the point, Plutarch claimed to know something about the Cymaean *basileis*. The citizens of Cyme, he said (*Quaest. Graecae* 2 = 291F–292A),

had an officer called a Guard. The man who held this office spent most of his time watching the prison. But entering the *boulē* in the nighttime session, he would lead the *basileis* out by the hand, and hold them until the *boulē*, voting by secret ballot, had decided whether they had done wrong or not.

60. *Herodotea Vita Homeri* (ed. T. Allen), ll. 123–89.
61. The epigram appears first in Plato *Phaedrus* 264C, who comments that "some say" that the epigram was inscribed on Midas' tomb.

The *basileis* in this passage are accountable—*hypeuthynoi*—which is to say that they are magistrates rather than kings.[62] Unfortunately, Plutarch does not give any chronological context for the practice that he describes. It is reasonably certain that during the Archaic period there was an aristocracy at Cyme. Aristotle knew of a *dokimos anēr* named Pheidon who had extended the Cymaean polity to all who could keep a horse, and of a *drastērios anēr*, Prometheus, who extended it to a thousand citizens.[63] Had there been a Cymaean *basileus* named Agamemnon, he would have been a magistrate within an oligarchical regime.

CONCLUSION

In no Greek city of the eastern Aegean, whether Ionian or Aeolian, is there evidence for kings in the Geometric period. In two of the Aeolian cities for which we have evidence, Mytilene and Cyme, we hear of a college of *basileis*, and probably in both cities the college already existed in the early Archaic period.

Our sources speak of no king at all in five of the twelve Ionian cities: Teos, Myus, Clazomenae, Lebedos, and Priene. In Hellenistic times three other cities—Erythrae, Colophon, and Phocaea—supposed that their oikists had been monarchs (or dyarchs, or triarchs), but assumed that such personal rule had ended with the oikists' generation. At Ephesus and Samos there were stories about the reign of the oikist's son. In Chios the several kings of whom Ion spoke were thought of as spanning the period from Theseus to the sons of Codrus. And at Miletus the Neleid monarchy was thought to have been abolished at the time that Branchus established his oracle at Branchidae.

Greek authors make no general statement that there were kings in the Ionian and Aeolian cities through most of their pre-Homeric history. No kinglists from these cities have survived, and there is no indication that such lists ever existed.

---

62. Monarchy and an *hypeuthynos archē*, as the Greeks saw it, were mutually exclusive. See Pausanias 4.5.10 and Herodotus 3.80.3.

63. Aristotle, fr. 611, no. 39 (Rose).

Late stories assume that the founder of a city ruled it, and that this personal rule disappeared because of an accident to the founder or to his son. Ionian and Aeolian traditions about early kings, therefore, seem to be nothing more than a facet of traditions about heroic founders: a founding hero could have been nothing less than a monarch, but after the hero's death a normal form of government was established.

SICILY AND MAGNA GRAECIA

There is no need to linger long in Western Greece. Only a few Greek colonies had been established in Italy and Sicily by the end of the Geometric period. In the Bay of Naples, the island of Pithecusae was perhaps settled by Chalcidians and Eretrians ca. 775 B.C., and on the adjacent shore Cumae was founded ca. 750 B.C. Naxos, Megara Hyblaea, Syracuse, Leontini, Catana, Zancle, and Sybaris were founded toward the end of the Geometric period, and the Spartan colony at Tarentum was planted at some time between 720 and 700 B.C.

The scarcity of Greek cities in the western Mediterranean during the Geometric period, however, is not the only reason for brevity. Historians have for the most part not imagined kings in any of the Western Greek cities. The conclusion of T. J. Dunbabin on this matter was that "the only possible West Greek king properly so titled is Aristophilides of Taras."[1] Many a tyrant who ruled in Sicily was addressed by his subjects or admirers as *basileus*, but that was a courtesy which has not misled ancient or modern observers. There are, as a matter of fact, only two individuals who have been seriously proposed as kings in a Western Greek city; in addition to Aristophilides, a shadowy figure named Pollis has from time to time been regarded as a king.

Tarentum   Aristophilides has the authority of Herodotus behind him. In the lengthy tale about Democedes, the physician from Croton, Herodotus tells how he contrived to be sent from

---

1. T. J. Dunbabin, *The Western Greeks* (Oxford: Clarendon, 1948), p. 385.

Susa back to his homeland: promising to lead fifteen distinguished Persians in a scouting mission through Greek waters, Democedes and the Persians requisitioned three ships at Sidon and began their coasting operation. Eventually

they arrived at Tarentum in Italy. There, out of compassion for Democedes, Aristophilides, the *basileus* of the Tarentines, first of all removed the rudders from the Median ships, and then he held the Perisans themselves on the pretense that they were spies. While the Persians were undergoing this ordeal, Democedes made his way to Croton. After Democedes had gotten back to his native city, Aristophilides freed the Persians and returned to them the rudders that he had removed from their ships. [Hdt. 3.136]

As we have seen, Herodotus' usage of *basileus* and *tyrannos* is consistent enough that we can exclude the possibility that Aristophilides was tyrant of Tarentum.[2] What kind of *basileia* was there in Tarentum ca. 515 B.C.?

As *basileus*, Aristophilides enjoyed enough power to initiate an action against the Persians' ships. We must conclude either that he was a king and the Tarentine state was a monarchy, or that as *basileus* he was the chief magistrate in a republic. On the basis of the very little that is known about Archaic Tarentum, the second alternative is the more likely. As Aristotle says (*Pol.* 1303a), shortly after the Persian Wars so many of the distinguished (*gnorimoi*) citizens of Tarentum died in battle against the Iapygians (ca. 473 B.C.) that what had been a *politeia* was changed into a *dēmokratia*. In Aristotle's lexicon, a *politeia* in the narrow sense is that form of government in which "the majority administers the state with a view toward the common good," whereas in a *dēmokratia* the state is administered for the benefit of the disadvantaged (*Pol.* 1279a–b). It is theoretically possible that the *politeia* to which Aristotle refers had been created between 515 and 473 B.C., and that prior to its creation Tarentum had been a monarchy. But there is another objection. A few paragraphs beyond his story of

2. See above, p. 27, n. 44.

Aristophilides and Democedes, Herodotus reports that the Persian spies were restored to Darius by a Tarentine exile named Gillus. To reward Gillus, Darius ordered the Cnidians (who were on unusually friendly terms with the Tarentines) to use their best offices to secure Gillus' return to Tarentum. Try as they might, however, the Cnidians "could not persuade the Tarentines" (Hdt. 3.138), and Gillus remained in exile. The decision, at least as reported by Herodotus, seems to have lain not with Aristophilides but with "the Tarentines," which suggests that Aristophilides was no monarch but instead was responsible to a council or assembly.

Since Tarentum was a Spartan colony, her *basileis* may have been of the Spartan variety. This possibility is enhanced by some indirect evidence that there were ephors at Tarentum.[3] Perhaps the Tarentine *basileis* were in charge of military, and quasi-military, operations while ephors administered the city's internal affairs.

Syracuse   King Pollis of Syracuse disappears on close inspection. Athenaeus, discussing the famous *biblinos* wine of Thrace (31a–b), says that according to Hippys of Rhegium, the vines which produced this wine were brought from Italy to Sicily by "Pollis the Argive, who reigned over the Syracusans" (ὃς ἐβασίλευσε Συρακοσίων). On this passage E. A. Freeman based a theory that the Syracusans, although initially governed by an aristocracy, at some point instituted a heroic monarchy.[4] That is unlikely. Pollis' identification as an Argive, whatever Athenaeus might have meant by the adjective, is apparently

3. For ephors at Tarentum see Pierre Wuilleumier, *Tarente des origines à la conquête romaine* (Paris: Boccard, 1939), pp. 176–77. In the fourth century annually elected *strategoi* led the Tarentine army. Wuilleumier suggests that the office of *strategos* was established, and the *basileia* abolished, in the democratization ca. 473 B.C.

4. E. A. Freeman, *History of Sicily* 4 vols. (Oxford: Clarendon, 1891), 2:8–10 and app. 1, pp. 431–36; Starr, "Decline of the Early Greek Kings," p. 134, n. 17, regarded Pollis as a real king and the original regime at Syracuse as a monarchy.

due to a conflation. For Julius Pollux (*Onom.* 6.16) distinguishes between an Argive Polis and a Syracusan Pollis:

And there is a sweet "Polis" wine." This is from Syracuse, and Polis the Argive first produced it and gave his name to it; or it may be named after Pollis the Syracusans' king, as Aristotle says.

Nor is Pollis' identification with Syracuse any more trustworthy. Aelian (*Var. Hist.* 12.31) also mentions the wine: "there is Pollis' wine at Syracuse. It received its name ἀπὸ δέ τινος ἐγχωρίου βασιλέως." That phrase can only mean "some native king":[5] Aelian did not suppose that Pollis was Syracusan at all. Dunbabin pointed out that Pollis was probably invented after the time of Epicharmus of Syracuse;[6] for in his discussion of *biblinos* wine Athenaeus cites Epicharmus, and the fifth-century Syracusan seems to have said nothing about Pollis. We may conclude with Dunbabin that "it seems most probable that Pollis king of Syracuse is an etymological fiction, invented in the fourth or third century to explain the name given in Sicily to the wine of the type elsewhere called Βίβλινος."[7]

Nobody else, of course, has been suggested as king of Syracuse before the metamorphosis of Agathocles. The oikist Archias is nowhere referred to as a king, and scholars are fairly well agreed that "il regime dello stato siracusano in quei primi tempi era, quasi certamente, un regime aristocratico o addirittura plutocratico: i *gamoroi*."[8] We may conclude that none of the states of Western Greece was ruled by a monarch in the eighth century. Tarentum undoubtedly had a *basileus* from the

5. By itself, ἐγχώριος might be translated "locally born," meaning that Pollis was by birth a Syracusan and not an Argive. The τινος, however, favors translating ἐγχώριος as "indigenous," i.e. as of native Sicel rather than of Greek stock. Cf. the ἐγχώριοι βασιλῆες of Pindar, *Ol.*9.56.

6. Dunbabin in *Western Greeks*, pp. 93–94 has a detailed appendix on Pollis.

7. *Western Greeks*, p. 94.

8. Alberto Fiori, *Siracusa greca* (Rome: Officina Edizioni, 1971), p. 18. Cf. Marie-Paule Loicq-Berger, *Syracuse: Histoire culturelle d'une cité grecque* (Brussels, 1967; = *Collection Latomus*, 87) pp. 34–35.

beginning, but he functioned within a *politeia*, in the narrow, Aristotelian sense of the word.

THE ISTHMUS AND PELOPONNESE

The belief that the Ionian cities had been founded by heroes from Nelian Pylos, we have seen, resulted in stories about heroic kings in several of the Ionian cities. In the Peloponnese the seminal myth was that of the Return of the Heraclidae. Although the earliest extant version of the full story appears in the *Bibliotheca* of Apollodorus, there is evidence that the story had taken shape in the Archaic period.[1] The early story seems to have been as follows.

After Heracles was translated to the gods, his sons were banished from the Peloponnese by Eurystheus, king of Mycenae or Argos. One of Heracles' sons, Hyllus, led his brethren back to the Isthmus, where he challenged the Peloponnesians to a Battle of Champions. The Heraclidae promised that if Hyllus were defeated they would retire and would not return for fifty, or some say a hundred years. As it happened, Hyllus was killed, and the Heraclidae therefore remained in the north for another fifty or one hundred years. Hyllus' grandson, Aristomachus, made another attempt, which also was unsuccessful, and it was left to Aristomachus' three sons to effect the Return. These three Heraclidae were Temenus, Cresphontes, and Aristodemus. Apollo told them that they would succeed, and that a three-eyed guide would lead them. They crossed the Corinthian Gulf near Naupactus and on the Peloponnesian side met a man—Oxylus son of Andraemon, an exile from Aetolia—riding a horse that was blind in one eye. Following him, the Heraclidae came up against the Peloponnesian army,

1. Apollodorus *Bibliotheca* 2.8. The myth was well known in Herodotus' day; Hdt. 6.52, where we find that although the poets had told how Aristodemus' two sons led the Dorians to Lacedaemon, the Spartans claimed that Aristodemus himself had brought them in. For a detailed study of the evolution of the myth see F. Kiechle, "Die Ausprägung der Sage von der Rückkehr der Herakleidai," *Helikon* 6 (1966):439–517.

led by Orestes' grandson (or son) Tisamenus, defeated it, and so regained the Peloponnese. The Argolid was awarded to Temenus, Lacedaemon to Aristodemus, and Messenia to Cresphontes. Eventually this myth included most of the Dorian communities in the Peloponnese. So, for example, the Corinthians claimed that the reputed founder of Dorian Corinth, Aletes (the common noun *alētēs* meant "wanderer"), was a grandson of Antiochus, son of Heracles, and fought side by side with the heroes of Argos, Sparta, and Messenia. Even the Dorian conqueror of tiny Phlius was usually counted as a Heraclid.[2] The myth of the Return of the Heraclidae must also be kept in mind as we analyze the evidence for kingship in non-Dorian states of the Peloponnese, for even those peoples who did not consider themselves Dorian organized their mythology around the Return.

Elis The single passage that tells of kingship in Elis is Pausanias 5.4.5. There we read that Oxylus, the three-eyed guide of the Heraclidae, founded and ruled Dorian Elis, and that he was succeeded by his son Laias. However, continues Pausanias, "I do not find that Laias' descendants were kings." As in many Ionian cities, the heroic founder and his son were assumed to have been kings, but it was also assumed that monarchy lapsed with the heroic age.

In the government of Archaic Elis, about which very little is known, a group of *basileis* apparently played a significant role. In an inscription of the sixth or early fifth century, a "rhetra of the Elians," τοι βασιλαες are responsible for some aspect of judicial procedure.[3]

---

2. J. Toepffer, s.v. Aletes, *RE* I, 1371, described the name Aletes (ἀλήτης) as "ein mythischer Ausdruck für die Wanderungen seines Stammes." On the Phliasians' traditions about Rhegnidas, son of Phalces and grandson of Temenus, see Pausanias 2.13.

3. For the inscription see L. H. Jeffery, *The Local Scripts of Archaic Greece* (Oxford: Oxford Univ. Press, 1961), Elis no. 15; the text appears on p. 408 and Professor Jeffery's comments on p. 218, esp. n. 5.

Achaea   The mountainous southern coast of the Corinthian Gulf between Elis on the west and Sicyon, a conventional polis, on the east, was an ethnic and geographical entity known as Achaea. Strung across its hundred-mile length were the twelve communities of the Achaean *koinon*, most of them little more than hilltop villages. Lying between two of these villages was a larger town, Patrae, which coexisted with the *koinon* and eventually joined it. Patrae had its own traditions of heroic kings: Preugenes and his son Patreus came from Lacedaemon (the Achaeans concluded from the *Iliad* that at one time the greatest of the Achaeans had lived in Argos and Lacedaemon), and of course Patreus founded Patrae.[4] Apparently the eponymous hero was regarded as the first and last king of Patrae.

Pausanias reports that when the Achaeans took over the twelve kindred towns, driving out the Ionians who had hitherto inhabited them, the *basileis* of the Achaeans were the four sons of Tisamenus, son of Orestes (the four were joined by a cousin, Damasias; he was a son of Penthilus, son of Orestes).[5] Polybius, who knew so much about third-century Achaea, knew very little about earlier Achaean history. He did have one generalization to make, and made it twice: at 2.41.4–5 he says,

Before this date [in other words, the 124th Olympiad, 284–80 B.C.], the condition of the aforementioned *ethnos* [in other words, the Achaean] was something like this: being ruled by kings from the time of Tisamenus, who was the son of Orestes, the Achaeans were driven out of Sparta at the time of the Return of the Heraclidae, and took over the places in Achaea; from Tisamenus on, in hereditary succession, they were ruled by kings until Ogygus. But then, being dissatisfied with the sons of the aforementioned, specifically at their ruling despotically rather than according to *nomos*, the Achaeans transformed their *politeia* into a democracy.

This democracy, according to Polybius, lasted until the time of Alexander. At 4.1.5 Polybius repeats his observation that from

4. Pausanias 7.6.2.
5. Pausanias 7.6.1–2.

Tisamenus to Ogygus there were kings of Achaea, all from the same *genos*, after which a democracy was installed. For good measure we have Strabo's repetition (8.7.1) of what he had read in Polybius' history.

Nothing else is known of Ogygus, and it has been suggested that he was a Hellenistic invention: if the first king of the Athenians was Ogygus (in whose time the Great Flood occurred), the last king of the Achaeans could also be an Ogygus.[6] There are no grounds for confidence that an Ogygus ever ruled in Achaea, but it must be noted that there was a tradition about post-heroic kings in Achaea: not only were the Achaeans ruled by a founding hero and his sons, as in Ionia, but they continued to be *basileuthentes* for some time after the heroic age.

Achaea was an *ethnos*, and it may be that its government during the Geometric period was somewhat different from that which obtained in the city-states. Aristotle, it will be recalled, remarked (*Pol.* 1252b) that the *poleis* had kings "initially," and that the *ethnē* had them "even now." Unlike Aristotle, I am not persuaded that most *poleis* were ever ruled by kings. But his remark must at least alert us to the possibility that an *ethnos* may have had a monarchy in post-heroic times. Some *ethnē* did not (in Elis, as we have just seen, no king was claimed after the founding hero's son), while others clearly did: the Macedonians are the most obvious example. Let us keep in mind the possibility that there were kings in Geometric Achaea.

Sicyon   The Sicyonian kinglist, after Castor of Rhodes had finished with it, reached farther back into the past than the kinglist of any other Greek city. Sicyon's first king, Aegialeus ("coastman"), father of Europs, was revealed to have come to the throne in our year 2123 B.C. This meant, Castor was pleased to tell the Greeks of his day, that Aegialeus was an exact contemporary of Belus, the most ancient of the barbarian

6. Wörner, s.v. Ogygos II, in Roscher *Lex.* III, 694.

kings.[7] Sicyon's twenty-six kings ruled for almost a thousand years; then, having served its purpose, the dynasty ended and there were no more kings in Sicyon other than the Heraclid hero who conquered it. Recording the death of Zeuxippus, the twenty-sixth and last pre-Dorian king of Sicyon, in the 889th year of Abraham (1128 B.C.), Jerome noted:

Reges Sicyonis defecerunt, qui regnaverunt ann. DCCCCLXII. Post quos Sacerdotes Carni constituti sunt.

A generation later Sicyon was captured by Phalces. Though he was a son of Temenus, Phalces was not a likeable figure. Temenus' sons, Phalces and Ceissus, were angered when their father preferred his daughter Hyrnetho and her husband Deïphontes to them; and so, with Phalces the moving spirit, they murdered their father. At that, the Epidaurians and Argives made Deïphontes and Hyrnetho king and queen. Phalces responded by abducting his sister from her husband and slaying her. (The place where Hyrnetho was buried by Deïphontes and their children was ever after a holy place for the Epidaurians.)[8]

The Sicyonians apparently accepted the story that Phalces was the Heraclid who had won their town for the Dorians. But they did not, understandably, suppose that thereafter Sicyon was ruled by a line of Phalcid kings. We hear, therefore, about no Sicyonian king after Phalces.

Corinth   For Corinth we have from Eusebius[9] a full roster of post-heroic kings, spanning the period from the Return to the eighth century. This kinglist, as I remarked in the introductory chapter, has powerfully abetted the general notion that during the Geometric period the Greeks were ruled by kings.

Paradoxically, the list has seldom been taken very seriously.

7. Castor (*F.Gr.Hist.* no. 250), fr. 1 and 2.
8. Pausanias 2.6.7 reports that Phalces and Lacestadas were colleagues in kingship at Sicyon. On Phalces see Apollodorus, *Bibliotheca* 2.172 and Pausanias 2.28. Hyrnatho was a goddess in both Argos and Epidaurus, and her name was reflected in the fourth Argive tribe, the Hyrnathioi. When she was demoted from goddess to daughter of Temenus is not known.
9. Eusebius, *Chron.* I, cols. 220–22 (Schoene).

George Grote called it "a mere barren genealogy."[10] Wade-Gery's verdict, in 1925, was even less generous:[11]

The names of the early kings of Corinth, from Aletes the founder, have been preserved by the ancient chronographers to whom they gave a framework of chronology down to the First Olympiad. The names are of no value.

And after making a detailed analysis of the Corinthian kinglist, Édouard Will characterized its names and numbers as "élucubrations où il semble qu'on perde sa peine à tenter de retrouver les linéaments d'une histoire."[12]

Even though the list's names and regnal periods are regarded as invented, or at least as unreliable, there is no tendency to doubt the existence of monarchy in early Corinth. The list as a whole, it seems, has a value quite independent of the sum of its parts. So, for example, Wade-Gery's comment continues thus:

But we need not doubt that there were kings in Corinth *as elsewhere*, and that in the eighth century they gave way before the aristocracy. [my italics]

In other words, the known but fictitious kings of the list have usurped the place of real but unknown kings. Similarly, though Édouard Will chose to begin his survey of early Corinth with the oligarchy, he accepted the tradition that the Bacchiads had ruled first as kings and then as oligarchs: "Le fait s'inscrit *dans l'évolution générale de la cité grecque* et nous ne disserterons pas sur *ce phénomène connu* du passage de la royauté au régime aristocratique" [my italics].[13]

Although the kinglist comes to us through Eusebius, who found it in the seventh book (now lost) of Diodorus, what we have are a Greek paraphrase and an Armenian translation of Eusebius. Despite its precarious transmission, the Diodoran text survives in a form that must be reasonably close to its original.

10. Grote, *History of Greece* 3:86.
11. Wade-Gery, "The Growth of the Dorian States," *CAH* III (1925), p. 534.
12. Édouard Will, *Korinthiaka* (Paris: Boccard, 1955), p. 280.
13. Will, *Korinthiaka*, p. 298.

At the Return of the Heraclidae almost all the nations of the Peloponnese, the Arcadians excepted, were driven from their homes. In dividing the land the Heraclidae made Corinth and the land around it a unit all its own, and sent word over to Aletes, handing over to him the area just described. Becoming a distinguished man, and having brought increase to Corinth, he was king for 38 years. After his death came his descendants, the oldest son always reigning, until the tyranny of Cypselus, which followed the Return of the Heraclidae by 447 years. The first among them to inherit the kingship was Ixion, for 38 years. After him Agelas ruled for 37, after them Prymnis for 35, and Bacchis for the same length of time, Bacchis being the most illustrious of the whole line up to that point. For this reason it happened that those who reigned afterwards were no longer called Heraclidae, but Bacchidae. After him came Agelas, for 30 years, Eudemus for 25, Aristomedes for 35. At his death he left a son Telestes, still just a child; the kingship, which by hereditary right belonged to the child, was taken by his paternal uncle and guardian, Agemon, who ruled 16 years. After him Alexander was in control for 25 years. Telestes, the one who had been cheated of his hereditary position, killed Alexander and ruled for 12 years. When he was killed by kinsmen, Automenes ruled for one year; and the Bacchidae, descended from Heracles, numbering more than two hundred, were in control of the *archē*, and all of them together were leaders of the polis, but of their number they chose one person each year as *prytanis*, who held the position of the king, for 90 years until the tyranny of Cypselus, by which they were brought to an end.[14]

Diodorus was obviously confused by what he found in his source. He states that for 447 years, from the Return until the tyranny of Cypselus, eldest son succeeded father on the throne; but by the end of the paragraph Diodorus has contradicted himself, stating that for the last ninety years of the span there were no longer kings, but annually elected *prytaneis*. Quite apart from that volte-face, the numbers do not add up to the required total. Of course, Eusebius or Syncellus may have cop-

---

14. Eusebius, *Chron.* I, cols. 219–22 (Schoene). The Armenian translation agrees closely with the Greek version from the Chronographia of the ninth-century Byzantine scholar Georgius, commonly called Syncellus. We can therefore be confident that we have approximately what Eusebius wrote.

ied the text incorrectly. Conveniently, however, in the Armenian translation of Eusebius we find that Eusebius went on to convert Diodorus' narrative into the form of a canon (thereby, incidentally, greatly enhancing its appearance of authority),[15] and the regnal periods in the canon match exactly the regnal periods which Eusebius attributed to the Corinthian kings in his second book, his columnar chronology of world history. Eusebius' canon of Diodorus' kings runs as follows:

Aletes	35
Ixion	37
Agelas	37
Prymnis	35
Bacchis	35
Agelas	30
Eudemus	25
Aristomedes	35
Agemon	16
Alexander	25
Telestes	12

Now Diodorus said that altogether there were 447 years from the Return to Cypselus' coup, and that for the last ninety years annual *prytaneis* were in control. That would mean that the kings ruled for 357 years. But when we add together the regnal periods of Diodorus' eleven kings, we come up with only 322 years. Obviously, one king has fallen out in the transfer from Diodorus' source to Diodorus. The source, in other words, must have posited a list of twelve Corinthian kings. The twelfth king, like so many others in this list, will have had a reign of thirty-five years.[16]

Since we learn from Diodorus that Cypselus became tyrant in 657 B.C., it is a simple matter to calculate that kingship ended in Corinth, and the ninety-year period of the *prytaneis*

---

15. Eusebius, *Chron.* I, col. 221 (Schoene).

16. For detailed discussions of Diodorus' Corinthian chronology see Busolt, *Griechische Geschichte* 1:631–33, n. 4; and Will, *Korinthiaka*, pp. 259–80.

began, in 747 B.C. Although most historians today are skeptical of Telestes and of every other name in the list of Corinthian kings, there is a readiness to believe the broad outlines of Diodorus' account: after several generations of kingship at Corinth, the royal clan abolished the kingship ca. 747 B.C. and put in its place an annual magistracy.

Let us test the authority of Diodorus' kinglist. We may begin by reviewing what other sources say about pre-Cypselid Corinth. Herodotus, our earliest authority, puts into the mouth of the Corinthian Socleës a single sentence on the subject.

For the Corinthians, the constitution [katastasis] of their polis was this: there are an oligarchiē, and those who were called Bacchiads administered the polis, and they married and gave in marriage only among themselves. [5.92.b,1]

Nowhere does Herodotus say anything about kings of early Corinth. How long the oligarchiē had been in existence Herodotus does not say, although of course his story assumes that it was running smoothly before Cypselus was born.

In the Augustan Age Nicolaus of Damascus[17] recounted Cypselus' coup, identifying "the Bacchiads" as Cypselus' opponents, and "them" as the object of the Corinthians' hatred. Yet Nicolaus has a king reigning, one Hippocleides (or Patrocleides), and presents Cypselus as dispatching this unpopular figure and becoming king in his stead. Apparently Nicolaus made no mention of an annual prytanis.

Another contemporary of Diodorus presents yet another pic-

---

17. Nicolaus (F.Gr.Hist. no. 90), fr. 57. Some have thought that Nicolaus' basileus was a synonym for prytanis, and that Nicolaus had got hold of a reliable tradition that in the year of Cypselus' coup the annual magistrate (whether titled basileus or prytanis) was named Patroclides. That is not impossible. The fragment reads: "Finally, gathering together a band of supporters, he (i.e., Cypselus) slays basileuonta Patrokleidēn, who was lawless and detested. And immediately, in place of him the demos made Cypselus basileus. Cypselus died after being basileus for thirty years." Whatever source Nicolaus may have been following, Nicolaus himself surely pictured Patroclides as a monarch.

ture. Strabo (8.6.20) gives the following summary of early Corinthian history:

The Bacchiads, having established their tyranny [tyrannēsantes], and being wealthy, numerous and of noble birth, maintained their power [archē] for about two hundred years,

after which Cypselus evicted them. Although Strabo is not explicit about the institutions through which they ruled, his description of the Bacchiads suggests an aristocratic rather than a monarchic regime, apparently for the entire "two hundred years" of their supremacy.

Nor surprisingly, Pausanias (2.4.4) has something to say on early Dorian Corinth. After identifying Aletes as the great-grandson of Antiochus, son of Heracles, Pausanias continues:

Aletes himself and his descendants reigned for five generations to Bacchis, the son of Prumnis, and, named after him, the Bacchidae reigned for five more generations to Telestes, the son of Aristodemus. Telestes was killed in hate by Arieus and Perantes, and there were no more kings, but Prytanes taken from the Bacchidae and ruling for one year, until Cypselus, the son of Eetion, became tyrant and expelled the Bacchidae.

This version of things is similar to that in Diodorus. Pausanias, however, seems to have in mind only ten royal generations, and he names Telestes' father Aristodemus rather than, as in Diodorus, Aristomedes. But the overall resemblance to Diodorus' account suggests a common ultimate source.

Finally, Eusebius supplies some so-called primary evidence on early Corinth. In addition to transmitting to us, in book one of the *Chronicle*, the Diodoran account already cited, Eusebius provides several dates for early Corinthian history in the second book of the *Chronicle*. Here we find, in the column reserved for the kings of Corinth, all of the names reported by Diodorus, the accession and death of each king being dated to the era of Abraham. In the year corresponding to 779 B.C. the death of the last Corinthian king is entered. "Post hos," we read in Jerome's Latin version of the *Chronicle*, "in Corintho constituti sunt annui prytanis." Since Cypselus' coup is dated to 659 B.C. in the *Chronicle*, one can deduce that there must have been one hundred and twenty of these annual *prytaneis*. All of our sources agree, and there is no reason to doubt, that before the tyranny of Cypselus Corinth was ruled by the Bacchiads. Who these Bacchiads were is less clear. Diodorus and Pausanias, of course, say that they got their name from the illustrious Bacchis. Scholars have usually regarded the Bacchiads as a clan, or a *genos*,[18] but such an interpretation is difficult to maintain after F. Bourriot's analysis of the early *genos*. It is more likely that the Bacchiads formed a caste, or a closed "governing class," perhaps analogous to the Eupatrids in pre-Solonian Athens.[19] It may be, as Diodorus reports, that the Bacchiads numbered slightly over two hundred men.

"All of them together," Diodorus continues, "were leaders of the polis, but of their number they chose one person each year as *prytanis*." Eusebius and Pausanias also attest to the annual *prytaneia*, but that need not mean very much: Eusebius depended on Diodorus, and both Pausanias and Diodorus may have depended on a common ultimate(though not immediate) source, probably Ephorus. Nicolaus' account has no room for a *prytanis*; and although Herodotus' short description of the Bac-

---

18. Cf. Jeffery, *Archaic Greece*, p. 145: "Traditionally in 747 a hereditary kingship ended when the royal clan . . . took over the rule of the city. This is a classic example of the earliest type of aristocracy, formed when the royal kin of an ineffective monarch took power from him, but kept it wholly in their hands."

19. On Bourriot's study see above, Introduction, n. 1. Karl-Wilhelm Welwei, "Adel und Demos in der frühen Polis," *Gymnasium* 88 (1981):10, finds Bourriot's argument persuasive ("der These vom sog. Geschlechterstaat als Vorstufe der Polis lässt sich nicht verifizieren") and uses it to dispute the usual identification of the Bacchiads as a *genos*, and their rule as a *Geschlechterherrschaft*. Welwei argues instead that the Bacchiads were "eine Gruppe von Adelshäusern . . . die die Macht monopolisiert hatten und durch ein genealogische Fiktion ihre Herrschaft zu legitimieren suchten. Auch in diesem Fall erwiest sich der Begriffe des Geschlechterstaates als problematisch. Ebenfalls abzulehnen ist die vor allem in der angelsächsischen Forschung vielfach übliche Bezeichnung der griechischen Adelshäuser als 'clans'."

chiad *oligarchiē* does not at all exclude the possibility of an annual *prytanis*, it does not mention such an officer.

Epigraphic evidence from the Corinthian colonies, however, lends strong support to Diodorus' account of a *prytaneia*. Inscriptions from the Hellenistic and Roman periods indicate a single annual *prytanis* at Corcyra, Epidamnus, Ambracia, and Apollonia (unfortunately, nothing is known about the magistracies of Archaic Syracuse), and it is likely that the institution was there from the outset of the colonies.[20] Ephorus, or whoever it was who first wrote about the Bacchiad *prytaneis*, apparently happened upon a reliable tradition.

That the regime of the Bacchiad *prytaneis* began ninety years before Cypselus' coup is not improbable. Eusebius placed the first *prytanis* in 779 B.C. rather than in 747 B.C., but he did so for chronographic reasons. Because he dated the Return thirty-two years earlier than Diodorus had, while raising the date of Cypselus' coup by only two years, Eusebius had to account for an extra thirty years between the Return and the coup. He did so by lengthening the regime of the *prytaneis* from ninety years to a hundred and twenty. Eusebius' dates for the beginning and end of the *prytaneia* therefore have no independent value. They do, however, indicate—what would reasonably have been supposed anyway—that there was no *list* of annual Corinthian magistrates available to Diodorus and Eusebius. There was only a figure, which could be manipulated to fit the chronographic system at hand.

Strabo declared that the Bacchiads maintained their rule— apparently an aristocratic regime—for about two hundred years. But Strabo's report inspires little confidence. That ca. 850 B.C. there were any wealthy individuals at Corinth, much less a whole aristocracy, is difficult to believe: what archaeologists have discovered about the Dark Age does not suggest the presence of a "wealthy, numerous" aristocracy in any Greek

---

20. The definitive article on the various *prytaneis*, whether the single magistrate or the board, is now Fritz Gschnitzer's, s.v. Prytanis, *RE Supplement* XIII, 730–816; on the *prytanis* in the Corinthian colonies see col. 737.

settlement in the middle of the ninth century.[21] The most likely explanation for Strabo's chronology is that he had heard that there were slightly more than two hundred members of the Bacchiad aristocracy, and that one Bacchiad served each year as *prytanis*. Without much intelligence, Strabo probably deduced that the Bacchiad regime had therefore lasted about two hundred years.

The *terminus ante quem* for the establishment of the Bacchiad aristocracy and the institution of the *prytaneia* should be the colonization of Corcyra, traditionally dated to 734 B.C. Since both Corcyra and her own colony, Epidamnus, had an annual *prytanis*, it seems that the *prytaneia* in Corinth was established well before the end of the eighth century. The Diodoran date of 747 B.C. may not be very far from the mark, and it is possible that the oral tradition which preserved the memory of the pre-Cypselid *prytaneia* also included a vague recollection of how long the regime had lasted.

Let us turn now to Diodorus' kings. His list certainly was given its final form late in the Hellenistic period, after Apollodorus had published his *Chronica*. The descendants of Aletes the Heraclid, according to Diodorus, reigned "until the tyranny of Cypselus, which followed the Return of the Heraclidae by 447 years." Diodorus' 447 years are the difference between Apollodorus' dates for the Return (1104 B.C.) and for Cypselus' coup (657 B.C.).[22] Once the datelists of Eratosthenes and Apollodorus had gained general acceptance, the lacunae between major events in each locality needed to be charted. Diodorus' source probably subtracted ninety years of *prytaneis* from the entire period of 447 years, and thus came up with 357 years for the monarchy. These 357 years he distributed among twelve kings.

21. For a summary of the evidence on Corinth see Carl Roebuck, "Some Aspects of the Urbanization of Corinth," *Hesperia* 41 (1972):103–05. For the wider picture see A. M. Snodgrass, *The Dark Age of Greece* (Edinburgh: Edinburgh Univ. Press, 1971), pp. 387–88.

22. Felix Jacoby, *Apollodors Chronik* (1902; reprinted, New York: Arno, 1973), pp. 77 and 152.

That there had been Heraclid kings in Corinth, however, was not an invention of the Hellenistic chronographer. Pausanias' slightly different account attributed ten generations of Heraclid kings and then the regime of the *prytaneis* to pre-Cypselid Corinth, and Pausanias must have been drawing on a source more elementary, and therefore earlier, than the chronographer. The first writer whom we know to have named Aletes was Ephorus, who made the Return the starting point and organizing principle of his history of the Peloponnese. Ephorus identified Aletes as the founder of Dorian Corinth,[23] and so presumably as its king. And if he spoke of a Heraclid monarch, Ephorus would also have had to explain how the monarchy gave way to the *oligarchiē* of the Bacchiads that Herodotus had reported. The story of Telestes, or something very much like it, was probably told by Ephorus.

The belief that Corinth had a Heraclid founder, finally, arose well before Ephorus' time. Thucydides (6.3.2) identified the oikist of Syracuse, Archias, as a Heraclid. For his *archaiologia* of Sicily, Thucydides seems to have drawn upon the Sicilian history written by Antiochus of Syracuse[24] soon after 424 B.C. It is perhaps not coincidental that the son of Heracles whose distant offspring Archias was reputed to have been, and through whom other Syracusans may have traced their Heraclid ancestry, was also named Antiochus. At any rate, we may be sure that Antiochus of Syracuse, late in the fifth century, advertised in his history that Syracuse had been founded by a descendant of Heracles. Once Corinth had been assigned a place in the story of the Return of the Heraclidae, later historians were left only with the task of finding the genealogical links between the heroic Antiochus and the historical Archias.

Nobody today, I think, believes that Dorian Corinth was founded by a descendant of Heracles. Along with their Heraclid

23. Ephorus (*F.Gr.Hist.* no. 70), fr. 18.
24. See Dover's discussion, pp. 201–02 in A. W. Gomme, A. Andrewes, and K. J. Dover, *A Historical Commentary on Thucydides,* 5 vols. (Oxford: Clarendon, 1970), vol. 4.

ancestry, the entire list of Corinthian kings must be dismissed. We are not dealing here with historical persons who have been made out to be descendants of a god, as for example the Julii of Rome were affiliated to Venus. What we have in Diodorus' eleven or twelve kings is a genealogical construction, intended to tie the Bacchiads to Heracles (as, for example, the Alban kings were presented as links between Aeneas and Romulus). That was not a deliberate fiction. The successive scholars who worked up the list of Corinthian kings had no reason to doubt that Dorian Corinth had been founded by a grandson of Heracles' grandson. And in bridging the gap between him and the Bacchiad *prytaneis* the ancient scholars were as resourceful and creative as paleontologists discovering the links between Australopithecus and Pithecanthropus. Ephorus undoubtedly mentioned the legendary figures that written and oral tradition supplied, and suggested where in the genealogy they might fit. The most familiar figures, and the least real, were Aletes ("the wanderer"), a personification of the Dorian migrants who settled at Corinth, and Bacchis, the eponymous hero of the Bacchiad aristocrats. Telestes may have been another personification, the "last king" of the line. Ixion, who was placed second in the list, immediately recalls the fabled Lapith who begat the race of Centaurs, and who still turns on a wheel in Hades. Cypselus claimed to be (or was said to have been) descended from a Lapith (Herodotus 5.92), and the claim may have provoked speculation about a Corinthian Ixion. By the time of the Apollodoran chronographer, enough names had been found or suggested to complete a series of eleven or twelve generations. But aside from Aletes, Bacchis and Telestes, the names were not the subjects of stories. Kings Eudemus, Agelas I, Agelas II, and the rest are not found outside the chronographic tradition, and did not become familiar to the world until Eusebius discovered them in Diodorus' *Bibliotheca* and featured them in his *Chronicle*.[25]

25. Eusebius especially needed Greek material for the period before the first Olympiad, and was well served by Diodorus' Corinthian kinglist. Otherwise, Eusebius had only the Athenian and Spartan lists with which to span the period from the Return to 776 B.C.

There was a time when Diodorus' list was taken seriously, even though *cum grano salis*, by philologists and historians. Several developments toward the end of the nineteenth century, among them the discovery of the Babylonian Chronicles (and the assumption that the early Greeks too must have compiled such records) and archaeologists' apparent vindication of some of the Greeks' heroic traditions, led a number of influential scholars to credit much of what fourth-century and Hellenistic writers said about early post-heroic Greece. Wilamowitz supposed that in the eighth century the Greeks began to compile written lists of kings and magistrates.[26] Like Wilamowitz, Eduard Meyer believed that as soon as the Greeks acquired the alphabet they began keeping records which would eventually be utilized by scholars of the late Classical and the Hellenistic periods. Thus he reasoned that although the first few entries in each of the various kinglists and genealogies might be mythical, from about 900 B.C. onward true names were remembered and recorded.[27] That the last Corinthian king was deposed "um 747 v. Chr."[28] was for Meyer a fact set down in writing soon after it occurred.

We now know that in Archaic Greece there was nothing comparable to the temple records of the ancient Near East, and that lists of kings and magistrates were not drawn up in Greece until the second half of the fifth century.[29] Diodorus' list of

---

26. Wilamowitz was the most influential advocate of the thesis that the Archaic Greeks composed chronicles, annals, and kinglists, but the opinion was shared by most historians and philologists of the time including Wachsmuth, Meyer, Busolt, and Schwartz. For a comprehensive criticism of the thesis, see Felix Jacoby, *Atthis* (Oxford: Clarendon, 1949), pp. 176–77 and especially the pertinent notes on pp. 352–54.

27. "Im allgemeine beginnen die geschichtlichen Namen überall ungefähr um 900 v. Chr. Natürlich hat dabei die beginnende Verwertung der Schrift mitgewirkt." Meyer states this opinion in the first edition of *Geschichte des Alterthums* 5 vols. (Stuttgart: Cotta, 1884–1902) 2:310, and did not change his mind. It is still there in the last edition of *Geschichte des Alterthums* (Stuttgart: Cotta, 1910–58), vol. 3, ed. H. E. Stier, p. 285, n. 1.

28. *Geschichte des Alterthums* 1st ed., 2:349.

29. See especially pp. 176–96, "The Alleged Pre-Literary Chronicles," in Jacoby's *Atthis*; on the astrological context within which the Babylonian

Corinthian kings is later than most: although a Heraclid founder of Corinth was claimed (at least by the Syracusan Antiochus) as early as the fifth century, the framework of the genealogy seems to have been erected by Ephorus, and the details were not completed until after Apollodorus' time. The list tells us something about the role of heroic legends in the fifth century, and something about scholarship in the Hellenistic period, but nothing about Geometric Corinth.

In summary, the evidence for kingship in Corinth is a genealogical and chronographic construction, instigated by the claim that Dorian Corinth had a Heraclid founder. We know only that prior to Cypselus' coup the Corinthians were governed by a Bacchiad aristocracy. It is very likely that their regime was headed by an annual magistrate whose title was *prytanis*, and it is probable that by 657 B.C. the regime had been in existence for about ninety years.

Megara   Despite the ancient Megarians' belief that they had no kings after the heroic age, most historians have assumed that they did. The only evidence on which this assumption rests is the presence of a *basileus* in the government of Archaic and Classical Megara. So, for example, Georg Busolt declared: "Dass in Megara ursprünglich ein Königtum bestand, ist mit Sicherheit daraus zu schliessen, dass der eponyme Beamte stets den Titel βασιλεύς führte."[30] Thirty years later, Ernst Meyer said much the same in his article on Megara:

Von den staatlichen Zuständen der ältesten Zeit wissen wir nur so viel, dass hier *wie sonst* ein Königtum bestand, was daraus folgt, dass der eponyme Beamte der historischen Zeit der Basileus ist. [my italics][31]

What the Megarians themselves thought about these things comes down to us in an aetiological story reported by Pausanias:

Chronicles were compiled, see Drews, "The Babylonian Chronicles and Berossus," *Iraq* 37 (1975), pp. 39–55.

30. *Griechische Geschichte* 1:221–22, n. 3.

In the city are graves of Megarians. They made one for those who died in the Persian invasion, and what is called the Aesymnium was also a tomb of heroes. When Agamemnon's son Hyperion, the last king of Megara, was killed by Sandion for his greed and violence, they resolved no longer to be ruled by one king, but to have elected magistrates and to obey one another in turn. Then Aesymnus, who had a reputation second to none among the Megarians, came to the god in Delphi and asked in what way they could be prosperous. The oracle in its reply said that they would fare well if they took counsel with the majority. This utterance they took to refer to the dead, and built a council chamber (*bouleutērion*) in this place in order that the grave of their heroes might be within it. [1.43.3]

That the Megarians should have invented a man named Aesymnus in order to account for the exotic synonym for their *bouleutērion* causes no surprise and is in fact evidence that the Aesymnium was ancient enough that all memory of what the word meant had disappeared.[32] From their story we may conclude that there were no traditions about post-heroic kings in Megara.

The government of Megara before Theagenes' tyranny can be only dimly perceived. The *basileus* to which Busolt and Meyer referred appears on several inscriptions from Classical Megara and her colonies; the existence of a *basileus* in Chalcedon suggests that the institution in Megara was at least as old as the founding of Chalcedon, in the middle of the seventh century.[33] In addition to the *basileus* and to the council that met in the Aesymnium, there may have been a polemarch in early Archaic Megara.[34]

31. Ernst Meyer, s.v. Megara, *RE* XV, 182.
32. For the etymology see A. Maanzmann, s.v. Aisymnētai, in *Kl. Pauly* I, 200.
33. For the *basileus* at Megara see *IG* VII, 1–15; for the Chalcedonian *basileus* see *GDI*, vol. 3, nos. 3054 and 3055.
34. S. I. Oost, "The Megara of Theagenes and Theognis," *CP* 68 (1973):186, argues for a polemarch on the basis of Pausanias 1.39.6 and 1.44.6. Pausanias 1.44.1 suggests that later Megarians thought of Orsippus as both a winner in the fifteenth Olympiad (720 B.C.) and a general (or possibly a polemarch). It is possible that the figures whom Pausanias calls polemarch and general bore the

Argos The Classical Argives advertised their government as a democracy. And, as R. A. Tomlinson has shown,[35] the little that our sources say about it supports that description. We hear of a sovereign assembly and of a *bola* (whether this council was chosen by lot or elected we do not know). Another body known simply as "The Eighty" is mentioned once by Thucydides, and shows up again on a third-century inscription. The magistrates late in the fifth century were called *artynai*, a term that probably was as generic as "magistrates." At the Battle of Mantinea (418 B.C.), the army was led by a board of five generals; this board continued to be of importance after the Classical period, for a third-century inscription dates a grant of citizenship by reference to the secretary of the council, and to the president of the board of generals.[36]

How and when this democratic government came into being is not clear. The disaster that Argos suffered at the hands of the Spartans in the Battle of Sepeia (494 B.C.) probably led to reforms of a democratic character, but it is possible that even in the sixth century the regime was more or less democratic. From ca. 575–550 B.C. come three inscriptions which mention *damiorgoi* as the chief magistrates of the city.[37] They apparently, though not certainly, constituted a college. One of the inscriptions enumerates some dedications made to Athena Polias, and names six *damiorgoi* who were in office when the dedications were made.[38] A second inscription refers to a

---

official title of *basileus.* At both Megara and her colonies *aisymnatai* are attested by inscriptions, but whether they formed a college of magistrates or were members of the council (Aesymnium) is not clear. See Maanzmann, s.v. Aisymnētai, *Kl. Pauly* I, 200, and Oost, "Megara," p. 186.

35. R. A. Tomlinson, *Argos and the Argolid* (Ithaca, N.Y.: Cornell Univ. Press, 1972), pp. 192–99; for a more detailed discussion see M. Woerrle, *Untersuchungen zur Verfassungsgeschichte von Argos im 5. Jahrhundert v. Chr.* (Munich: München Komm. für alte Geschichte, 1964).

36. For references see Tomlinson, *Argos*, p. 273, nn. 5–12.

37. The dates are discussed by Jeffery, *Local Scripts*, pp. 156–58.

38. *SEG* XI, no. 314.

damiorgos (in the singular) who was responsible for carrying out the punishment for certain capital crimes.[39] The third inscription begins with the phrase, "nine *damiorgoi* were ruling," and then lists nine names.[40] It is possible that the nine represent a series of annual magistrates, but it is more likely that all nine were in office when the inscription was made.[41] At any rate, it is clear from this third inscription that the *damiorgoi* were, in the second quarter of the sixth century, the heads of the Argive state.

Yet in the Archaic period and through the first half of the fifth century there was also a *basileus* in the Argive government. Epigraphic evidence comes from ca. 450 B.C., in the form of a treaty that Argos made with Cnossus and Tylissus in Crete.[42] The inscription closes with the formula, "the stele was erected when Melantas was *basileus*. Lycotadas of the tribe Hylleis was presider." Herodotus (7.149) also referred to an Argive *basileus* in the fifth century. When the Spartans solicited Argos' assistance against the impending invasion by Xerxes' hordes, the Argives refused to cooperate unless they were given an equal share of the command. The Spartans, continues Herodotus, replied

that they had two *basileis*, but the Argives had one. Now it could not be that either of the Spartan *basileis* be deprived of the command, but nothing would prevent the Argive from having one vote to go along with the two Spartan votes.

The Argives of course found this unacceptable, and decided to sit out the invasion. Herodotus' story assumes that his public

---

39. *SEG* XI, no. 302 = *IG* IV, no. 506.

40. *IG* IV, no. 614, augmented by *SEG* XI, no. 336; cf. also *SEG* XVIII, no. 147.

41. N. G. L. Hammond, "An Early Inscription at Argos," *CQ* 54 (1960):33–36.

42. M. N. Tod, *A Selection of Greek Historical Inscriptions* 2nd ed., vol. 1 (Oxford: Clarendon, 1946), no. 33; Meiggs and Lewis, *Greek Historical Inscriptions*, no. 42.

had heard about the Argive *basileia*, and strongly suggests that the duties of that office included command of the Argives when they marched into battle.

The Argive *basileus* best known to ancients and moderns was Pheidon.[43] Though later authors dated Pheidon to the pre-Homeric period, Herodotus regarded him as a slightly older contemporary of Cleisthenes, tyrant of Sicyon at the beginning of the sixth century.[44] Ephorus made Pheidon the "tenth from Temenus," and may not have intended to move Pheidon significantly deeper into the past.[45] Ephorus had read in Herodotus' *Histories*, after all, that in each of the two royal houses at Sparta there were only sixteen *basileis* from the Return through the Persian Wars. And he may therefore have believed that the tenth generation after Temenus was approximately where an older contemporary of Cleisthenes of Sicyon belonged.[46] It was in Theopompus' *Philippica*, published in the 340s B.C., that Pheidon began to drop precipitously back through the centuries: Theopompus set Pheidon in the fifth generation from Temenus.[47] In the third century, the chronographer of the Parian Marble dated Pheidon's accomplishments to our year 894 B.C. (Eusebius' *Chronicle* steers between

---

43. The most persuasive handling of the evidence concerning Pheidon's dates and accomplishments can be found in Thomas Kelly's *A History of Argos to 500 B.C.* (Minneapolis: Univ. of Minnesota Press, 1976), pp. 94–129. The widely held early seventh-century date for Pheidon's acme, to which I also subscribed in print, is clearly wrong.

44. Hdt. 6.127.

45. Ephorus (*F.Gr.Hist.* no. 70), fr. 115.

46. For Herodotus' Spartan lists see 7.204 and 8.131. Ephorus placed Pheidon three generations after Lycurgus, and two generations after the foundation of Sicilian Naxos and Megara Hyblaea (Ephorus fr. 137 and 173).

47. Theopompus (*F.Gr.Hist.* no. 115), fr. 393 = Diodorus 7.17 = Syncellus 499.5. Truesdell S. Brown, *The Greek Historians* (Lexington, Mass.: D. C. Heath and Co., 1973), p. 116, concludes that 377 B.C. for Theopompus' birth, the date given by Photius, is approximately correct. Theopompus wrote his *Philippica* after finishing the *Hellenica*.

the extremes, dating Pheidon to 796 B.C.; that Pheidon flourished in 668 B.C. is entirely a modern invention).[48]

Herodotus described Pheidon not as a *basileus* but as a tyrant, who surpassed all other Greeks in hubris, who devised the Peloponnesians' system of measurements, and who took Olympia away from Elis in order personally to preside at the Games. His son Leocedes, according to Herodotus, was one of the suitors for the hand of Agariste, daughter of Cleisthenes of Sicyon.[49] There is no doubt that Pheidon was remembered only because he was a tyrant, and did extravagant things. He seems to have begun, however, as a *basileus*. Ephorus refers to him only as a *basileus*, and Aristotle says that "Pheidon at Argos and other tyrants came to power because they already had the *basileia*."[50] It would appear, therefore, that in the late seventh century Pheidon was the *basileus* at Argos, undoubtedly in command of the hoplites, and that he used this position to make himself tyrant of Argos.

A slightly earlier *basileus* is mentioned by Pausanias in his book on Messenia (4.35.2). The chronological context for this *basileus* is the aftermath of the Messenian Revolt (probably the third quarter of the seventh century), and we may therefore have more confidence in him than in the wraiths whom Pausanians associated with the Return or with the foundation of Ionian cities. Pausanias reports that because the Nauplians were friendly to Sparta, the Argives evicted them from Nauplia "when Damocratidas was the *basileus* in Argos" (Δαμοκρατίδα βασιλεύοντος ἐν Ἀργει), and to the refugees the Spartans gave the Messenian city of Mothone. Elsewhere

---

48. Parian Marble = *F.Gr.Hist.* no. 239. Kelly, *History of Argos*, p. 94, comments on the date 668 B.C.: "The most widely accepted date for Pheidon—the early half of the seventh century—rests on no ancient evidence at all, but rather on a nineteenth-century emendation of the text of Pausanias." The original text dates Pheidon's usurpation of the Olympic presidency to 748 B.C. (Paus. 6.22.2).

49. Hdt. 6.127.

50. Aristotle *Pol.* 1310b.

(4.24.4) Pausanias places the gift soon after the Messenian Revolt. Damocratidas could have been remembered because he commanded the Argives when they evicted the Nauplians, or because he was *basileus* for a long enough time that he could serve posterity as a chronological marker, or because he both commanded the troops and was a long-tenure *basileus*.[51]
There may also have been an Argive *basileus* in the late eighth century. When the Spartans under Nicander (usually dated to the second half of the eighth century) invaded the Argolid, they were aided, Pausanias says (2.36.4), by Asine; and therefore, after the Spartans had withdrawn, "the Argives and their *basileus*, Eratus," marched against and destroyed Asine. Although philo-Laconism was very likely not the reason for Asine's destruction, archaeological evidence indicates that the town was destroyed ca. 720 B.C.[52] There is no ostensible reason why a *basileus* named Eratus should have been invented for this occasion, and it would be safest to imagine that in the late eighth century the Argives were led into battle by a *basileus*.
We may conclude that through most of the Archaic period a single *basileus* was an important official at Argos. Although *damiorgoi* were the "rulers" of the city, the *basileus* seems to have been the city's military commander. There are several indications that the *basileus* inherited his position and held it for life. We have already seen that Damocratidas apparently served as a chronological marker for later generations, and so probably held his office for more than an annual term. And we

---

51. Busolt, *Griechische Geschichte* 1:625, n. 2, assumed that Damocratidas' office was annual, and that Pausanias' information came "aus einer annalistischen . . . argolischen Chronik." The belief that the Archaic Greeks kept chronicles, which muddied much nineteenth-century scholarship on Archaic Greece, was exploded by Jacoby's *Atthis*. Damocratidas must have survived in oral tradition.

52. Thomas Kelly, "The Argive Destruction of Asine," *Historia* 16 (1967): 422–31. That Sparta and Argos were enemies in the eighth century was Ephorus' inference from sixth-century circumstances. See Kelly, *History of Argos*, pp. 49–50 and 64–65, and Kelly's "The Traditional Enmity between Sparta and Argos: The Birth and Development of a Myth," *American Historical Review* 75 (1970):971–1003.

shall shortly see that in the fourth century Ephorus regarded the Argive *basileia*, then defunct, as a hereditary position: he reported that for a span of thirteen generations the Argive *basileia* passed from father to son. The Argive *basileia* seems to have been abolished soon after the middle of the fifth century. The latest Argive *basileus* known to us is Melantas, mentioned on an inscription of ca. 450 B.C. In Thucydides' details (5.58–79) on the Battle of Mantinea in 418 B.C. there is no reference to a *basileus*, and a board of five generals is in command of the Argive troops. Finally, a recently discovered Argive inscription from the late fifth century also implies that by that time the office of *basileus* had been discontinued: at the head of a list of war casualties are named various officials who fell in the war, and among them are an *iareus*, a *stratagos*, a *mantis* and—the important figure for our purposes—a *probasileus*. Ch. Kritzas, the epigrapher who has published this inscription, has canvassed four possible meanings of the title *probasileus* and has concluded that the title most likely describes an official who is "in the place of" or "instead of" the *basileus*. The *probasileia*, Kritzas reasonably suggests, was a diminished version of the earlier *basileia*.[53] Taken together, we may conclude that the last Argive *basileus*, and so the last lifetime commander of Argos' troops, may have been Melantas. By the late fifth century the *basileus* had been replaced by *stratagoi* and, it now appears, by a *probasileus*, who in all likelihood was an annual official.

Let us now turn from the real *basileis* of the Archaic period and the fifth century to see whether descendants of Heracles ruled as kings in Geometric Argos. The sad tale of the Temenids was already elaborated in the fifth century, for Eu-

---

53. For the inscription and commentary see C. B. Kritzas, "Κατάλογος πεσόντων ἀπὸ τὸ Ἄργος," pp. 497–510 in ΣΤΗΛΗ. ΤΟΜΟΣ ΕΙΣ ΜΝΗΜΗΝ Ν. ΚΟΝΤΟΛΕΟΝΤΟΣ (Athens, 1980). Kritzas does not challenge the common assumption that the fifth-century *basileus* in Argos was an annual, eponymous official. I would suggest that the inscription strongly supports the thesis that the fifth-century *basileus* was Argos' military commander.

ripides based a tragedy upon it.[54] We have seen that after Temenus had been awarded the Argolid as his domain, he was
slain by his sons Phalces and Ceisus. The former went on to
kill their sister Hyrnetho, who was thenceforth worshipped by
the Argives and especially by the Epidaurians, and both sons
were in the end exiled from Argos. The myth thus explained
for fifth-century Argives how the Heraclids had recovered the
land, and why the heroic dynasty had disappeared.[55]

Plato reflects this early version of the myth. He observed
that the Heraclids of Argos and Messenia had lost their kingship because they were too despotic, and he contrasted the fate
of these two houses with the career of the third Heraclid house,
the Spartan.[56] Plato supposed that the Argive and Messenian
Heraclids had been despots before the time of Lycurgus, and
that it was the extinction of these two monarchies that in-
spired Lycurgus to trim the prerogatives of Sparta's two kings,
and so to ensure their survival. Although Plato does not say
how many generations the Heraclids ruled in Argos and Messenia, it is not impossible that the despots he had in mind were
Ceisus and Polyphontes, the wicked Heraclid who slew
Cresphontes and usurped the Messenian throne.[57] If Plato did
envisage more than two Heraclid kings of Argos, he obviously
cannot have believed that kingship there continued long after
the heroic age.

In the Ionian cities, even during the Hellenistic and Roman
periods the myths continued to describe a heroic kingship of
one or two generations. At Argos the matter was unclear, for by
the end of the fourth century some Greeks, at least, no longer
considered the Temenid monarchy a short-lived institution.
The most important innovation was the casting of Pheidon as a

54. On Euripides' version see M. Mayer, s.v. Temenos, *RE* V[2], 438–39.
55. Nicolaus (*F.Gr.Hist.* no. 90), fr. 30. In Ephorus' version, as we shall see,
Ceisus returns and seizes the monarchy.
56. Plato *Laws* 690D–E; cf. *Epist.* VIII, 354B.
57. At *Laws* 690D–E, where Plato says that Temenus' poor legislation al-
lowed the kingship to become a tyranny, several generations of kings may be
envisaged. At *Epist.* VIII, 354B, we read that the Heraclid family destroyed
itself and the Argive polis, and that calls Ceisus to mind.

descendant of Heracles. Herodotus had called him a tyrant, and a paragon of hubris. For Ephorus, on the other hand, Pheidon was not a tyrant but a Heraclid king, in the tenth generation from Temenus. Ephorus gave currency to, though he hardly invented, the apologia that Pheidon's usurpation of the Olympic festival was not hubris at all: the Heraclid king was merely recovering the sites that Heracles had once won for himself.[58] The Argives undoubtedly preferred to describe their tyrant as motivated by *pietas* rather than as a lawless disrupter of panhellenic shrines.

But in order to accept such a version of Pheidon's career, Ephorus had to show that kingship did not in fact come to an end with the infamous Ceisus. The explanation that Ephorus gave comes to us through Pausanias:

> But from earliest times the Argives have loved freedom and self-government, and they limited to the utmost the authority of their kings, so that to Medon, the son of Ceisus, and to his descendants was left a kingdom that was such only in name. Meltas, the son of Lacedas, the tenth descendant of Medon, was condemned by the people and deposed altogether from the kingship. [2.19.2]

Thus Ephorus revealed that after Ceisus came Medon ("ruler") and a whole line of fainéant Heraclids who had a *basileia* in name only, Pheidon being the one exception. Lacedas can be none other than the son of Pheidon, and the unsuccessful suitor of Agariste; and the deposed Meltas, in this reconstruction, is Pheidon's grandson (as Pheidon was tenth from Temenus, so Meltas was tenth from Medon). The deposition of Meltas, whom Ephorus identified as the last king of Argos, was fixed by a chronographer (Diodorus 7.14) 549 years after the accession of Temenus.[59] That Lacedas and Meltas were in fact *basileis* in

---

58. Ephorus (*F.Gr.Hist.* no. 70), fr. 115.
59. The fragment (Diod. 7.14 = John Malalas, p. 68) does not name the Temenid dynasty, and says only that the *basileia* at Argos lasted 549 years. A. Andrewes, "Ephoros Book I and the Kings of Argos," *CQ* 45 (1951), arguing that Argive kingship lasted from the Dorian occupation to the middle of the seventh century, suggested that the 549 years referred not to the Temenid dynasty but to Inachus' heroic dynasty.

sixth-century Argos is perhaps a remote possibility, though it is far more likely that Ephorus deduced their positions and their relationship to each other. One can hardly avoid the suggestion that Ephorus' Meltas is a badly distorted recollection of Melantas, who appears as *basileus* in the treaty of ca. 450 B.C., and who may very well have been the last Argive *basileus*. The circumstances which led to the deposition of Ephorus' Meltas fit very well with the war which Argos and Tegea fought against Sparta in the 450s B.C.[60] That Ephorus could have so confused the past is not at all unlikely. There is no indication that before Ephorus' time anyone had written a history of Argos. Undoubtedly there was an oral tradition, in the fourth century, telling how the *basileia* was abolished because of the knavery of "Meltas" during a war with Sparta. But Ephorus may have been quite unable to determine when this war had occurred, and he may have been able to come up with no other Argive *basileus* later than Pheidon's son Lacedas. In such case, "Meltas" would necessarily have been set down as a son of Lacedas and grandson of Pheidon.

Although Ephorus had presented Pheidon as a Heraclid king of Argos, and the tenth lineal descendant from Temenus, there is no reason to think that Ephorus provided his readers with names for the seven generations that intervened between Medon and Pheidon. In order to compose a coherent history Ephorus had to systematize and organize the names that he

60. Diodorus 7.13, undoubtedly taken from Ephorus, reports that "the Argives and their *basileus*" suffered reverses in war with the Spartans, and that in its aftermath the Argives expelled their *basileus*. The *basileus* had turned over some Argive lands to the Arcadians during the war, and therefore he spent his exile at Tegea, where he was an honored guest. Although this Diodoran story might fit into sixth-century history, it fits just as well in the middle of the fifth century. The thirty-year peace treaty which Argos and Sparta negotiated in 451 B.C. ended a war in which Argos and Tegea, along with other Arcadians, had been allies. Herodotus (9.35.2) mentioned Sparta's "battle at Tegea against the Tegeates and Argives" in a digression on the seer Teisamenus, but Ephorus apparently did not know of it (it is not mentioned by Diodorus). Of Herodotus 9.35.2 Tomlinson, *History of Argos*, p. 269, n. 8, says "presumably this reference was overlooked by the fourth century historians."

received, but he does seem to have proposed names simply to fill a gap. However, very soon after Ephorus had written about Pheidon and early Peloponnesian history, pressure developed in another quarter to identify the Temenid ancestors of Pheidon. The Macedonian royal house had long considered itself descended from Heracles; and when Macedon under Philip II began to become dominant in the Aegean, the Greek world needed to know how this descent had come about. Herodotus had told (8.137–39) how three boys, vaguely identified as descendants (*apogonoi*) of Temenus, had gone off together to Macedon when they were exiled from Argos. And Herodotus had explained that Perdiccas, the youngest of the three, after several miraculous adventures became the founder of Macedon's royal Argead house: Perdiccas, Argaeus, Philippus, Aeropus, Alcetas, Amyntas, and Alexander were the seven Heraclid kings of Macedon before Xerxes' invasion. Like Herodotus, Thucydides (2.99.3) accepted the Macedonian kings' claim that they were "originally Temenidae from Argos." And in a play written for the pleasure of Archelaus of Macedon (reigned 413–399 B.C.), Euripides told how a son of Temenus, appropriately named Archelaus, came to Macedon, won the throne, and initiated the Heraclid line.[61]

It was well and good for Herodotus to tell a charming *logos,* or for Euripides to write a play about how a Temenid came to be king of Macedon. But a sophisticated historian such as Theopompus, writing when Macedon was a great power, was obliged to come up with something more serious. Accordingly, Theopompus presented a complete genealogy of the first Heraclid king of Macedonia. This Heraclid, according to Theopompus, was neither Herodotus' Perdiccas nor Euripides' Archelaus, but Caranus, who came from Argos with an army and conquered Macedon. And Caranus' father, reported Theopompus, was none other than Pheidon. Theopompus presented the

---

61. A. Nauck, *Tragicorum Graecorum Fragmenta* 2nd ed. (Leipzig, 1889), fr. 426ff.

following genealogy for the Macedonian royal house (the Argive links in Theopompus' chain are identified by italics):[62]

Heracles
Hyllus
Cleodaeus
Aristomachus
Temenus
Cissius
Thestius
Merops
Aristodamidas
Pheidon
Caranus
Coenus
Tirimmus
Perdiccas
(etc., as in Herodotus)

We note here that Pheidon is placed fifth from Temenus. Pheidon's predecessor, Aristodamidas, may have been inherited by Theopompus: Pheidon's patronymic was probably reported by Ephorus. As far as we know, Theopompus did not assign dates or regnal periods to his Temenids, but if we should wish to convert his genealogy into a chronology, we would have to place his Pheidon before 900 B.C., a far cry from the period in which Herodotus thought he lived. (Theopompus and the chronographer of the Parian Marble, who dated Pheidon to 894 B.C., were apparently not concerned that if he lived so early Pheidon could have done none of the things that made him famous: usurping the presidency of the Olympic festival which was founded in 776 B.C., introducing coinage, having a son who wooed Agariste.)

Another historian, followed by the Byzantine Georgius Syncellus at 499.12, presented the same Macedonian *Urkönig*, Caranus, with an Argive ancestry that did not include Pheidon,

---

62. Theopompus (*F.Gr.Hist.* no. 115), fr. 393 = Diodorus 7.17.

and was otherwise made up of names entirely different from those announced by Theopompus. A third version of the Macedonians' Temenid ancestors, also omitting Pheidon, was offered by Satyrus, a third-century Peripatetic. Let us set these various lists side by side:[63]

Theopompus	Satyrus	Syncellus 499.12
Temenus	Temenus	Temenus
Cissius	Ceisus	Lachares
Thestius	Maron	Deballus
Merops	Thestius	Eurybiades
Aristodamidas	Acous	Cleodaeus
Pheidon	Aristodamidas	Poeas
Caranus, etc.	Caranus, etc.	Caranus, etc.

For the Macedonians, any one of the detailed lists was undoubtedly more satisfactory than Herodotus' vague identification of Perdiccas as "a descendant of Temenus," or Thucydides' statement that the Macedonian kings were "originally Temenidae from Argos." For us, however, the lists are important for other reasons. First of all, they raise questions about Greek historiography. Was there any connected account of Argive history before Ephorus and Theopompus wrote?[64] Did somebody tell Theopompus that Caranus' father was Pheidon, or did Theopompus decide that matter on his own, despite the fact that it required him to date Pheidon several centuries earlier than Herodotus had? The listmakers, needing to show the Temenid ancestry of the Macedonian kings, certainly resorted to deductions, educated guesses, and undoubtedly to invention (needless to say, the Temenids which our three ge-

63. For the lists of Satyrus and Syncellus' other source see Jacoby's commentary on Theopompus fr. 393.
64. Tomlinson, *History of Argos*, p. 105, observes that "it would seem that the history of Argos was not properly recorded at all at least until the fourth century B.C. It is not surprising that our knowledge of Argive history is so scrappy and confused."

nealogists contributed to Argive history appear nowhere else in ancient literature). The entire operation was somewhat careless, even slipshod. When the third- and second-century chronographers translate the Macedonian kinglist into years, we discover that Herodotus' seven kings rule for 275 years, and that the three kings whom Theopompus had inserted at the far end—Caranus, Coenus, and Tirimmus—ruled for 78 years, thus placing Caranus' accession in 813 B.C.[65] And that—ten kings spanning 353 years—was stretching things to the utmost. At the other end, the chronographers' date for Temenus and the Return is 1104 B.C. There are just under three centuries between Temenus and Caranus' accession, and Theopompus hoped he had sufficiently bridged the gap by coming up with five names. Satyrus did no better; and Syncellus' other source, with six names, improved on things only slightly. Theopompus wrote before chronography had become an exact science, but it is no surprise that the Hellenistic chronographers could not use his or anyone else's post-heroic Argive kinglist: each king in the list would need to be assigned between fifty and sixty regnal years, and since each king was supposedly father to his successor, the scheme was beyond biological possibility.

That the lists of Argive Heraclids composed by Theopompus and later historians can supply us with information about Geometric Argos is a notion that need not be entertained. However, in rejecting the lists as fourth- and third-century constructions, we must not forget that Theopompus and his fellows were to some extent justified in compiling the lists. If everyone knows that the house of Philip is descended from Heracles, via Temenus and his Argive offspring, then as historian of Macedon one has a responsibility to come up with specific names for the genealogy. Given the "facts" that Theopompus inherited, it is not remarkable that the historian felt obliged to forge the missing links in the chain.

---

65. This is the date given in the second book of Eusebuis' *Chronicle* (there is no serious discrepancy here between the Armenian translation and Jerome's Latin version). See also Euseb. *Chron.* I, col. 227 (Schoene).

For our purposes, the lists are important primarily because they have an implication for the Argive *basileia* of the years 720–450 B.C. We have noted that the references to the several *basileis* during that period suggest, though they do not prove, that the position of the *basileis* was hereditary and tenured. The creation of the lists supports that suggestion. There was surely a presupposition in the middle of the fourth century that Pheidon had been in power all his life, and that he had inherited his position. And Ephorus' presentation of Lacedas and Meltas as Pheidon's heirs suggests that as far as fourth-century Greeks knew, there were hereditary *basileis* after Pheidon. Here we may look at one last story about the Argive *basileia*. Plutarch tells how, when the Heraclid *genos* became extinct, an oracle promised to the Argives that an eagle would select their next *basileus*.[66] The god fulfilled his promise when, several days later, an eagle swooped down from the sky and sat on the roof of Aegon's house. And so Aegon was selected to be *basileus*. Though many of us will not believe in the eagle, and may even have doubts about Aegon, it must be conceded that Plutarch's source did not think of the post-Heraclid *basileus* at Argos as an annual official. Taken together, the evidence points to a hereditary and lifelong *basileia* in Argos during the Archaic period and the first half of the fifth century.

Arcadia   "The Arcadians say that Pelasgus was the first inhabitant of this land. It is natural to suppose that others accompanied Pelasgus, and that he was not by himself, for otherwise he would have been a king without any subjects to rule over" (Pausanias 8.1.4). This amazing deduction reminds us that our source on Arcadian kings, Pausanias, was a man of enormous curiosity but limited intelligence. The entire section on early Arcadia (8.1.4–6.1) contains so many examples of his wonderful credulity that when one finally reaches his account of post-heroic kings, one is prepared to disbelieve anything that might be said about them.

---

66. Plutarch *de fort. Alex.* 8 = 340C.

Since the *Iliad* had reported that the Arcadians who went to Troy were led by Agapenor, son of Ancaeus, Pausanias naturally heard from the Arcadians that they had once been ruled by Ancaeus and Agapenor. Then, however, came a new dynasty:[67] "when Agapenor did not return home from Troy, the kingdom devolved upon Hippothoüs, the son of Cercyon. . . . No remarkable event is recorded of his life, except that he established as the capital of his kingdom not Tegea but Trapezus" (8.5.4). Hippothoüs' more famous son, Aepytus, entered the sanctuary of Poseidon at Mantinea, which no mortal should do, and as punishment was struck blind and died.

Aepytus is of considerable interest. The Catalogue of Ships, the oldest piece of Greek literature that has come down to us, describes Agamemnon's Arcadian allies as dwelling "near the tomb of Aepytus" (*Il.* 2.603). We may therefore suppose that in Dark Age Arcadia Aepytus was remembered and his tomb was pointed out.[68] It is probable that by the time the Arcadians of the late eighth century learned, from the *Iliad*, of Ancaeus and Agapenor, a genealogy for Aepytus was already current; and so it was deduced that Agapenor had died at Troy, without heirs.

Aepytus' son, according to Pausanias, was Cypselus. A succession of Cypselidae, ending after the great war between Sparta and Messenia, is reported by Pausanias, with occasional reports of catastrophic events that occurred under this or that king. In the reign of Simus, for example, the ancient wooden image of Black Demeter burned. The last of the Cypselidae was reputed to have been Aristocrates, whose daughter eventually became the mother-in-law of Periander (Diog. Laert. 1.94). This Aristocrates was stoned to death when the Arcadians dis-

---

67. *Iliad* 2.609. On the two Arcadian dynasties—heroic and post-heroic—see F. Hiller von Gaertringen, "Pausanias' arkadische Königsliste," *Klio* 21 (1927):1–13.

68. That is not to say that a man named Aepytus was once king of Arcadia and was buried in the tomb. We are dealing here with a popular tradition. Whether the Aepytus in the tomb was "the same person" as the Aepytus who was struck blind, or the Aepytus who was poisoned by a snake, is ontologically unanswerable.

covered that he had betrayed the Messenians to Sparta in the disaster at the Great Ditch. "This sin," Pausanias reports, "explains why the kingship was taken from the whole house of Cypselus (8.5.13)." Let us list Pausanias' Cypselid kings:

Cypselus
Holaeas
Bucolion
Phialus
Simus
Pompus
Aeginetes
Polymestor
Aechmis
Aristocrates
Hicetas
Aristocrates

The list may contain a doublet and two unlikely eponyms, Phialus and Cypselus himself. The historicity of the dynasty as a whole is less suspect. Of his list Pausanias says (8.6.1) "I spent much care upon the history of the Arcadian kings, and the genealogy as given above was told me by the Arcadians themselves." In other words, this was not a dynasty worked out by a chronographer or a historian who needed to bridge a gap, but was part of what we may call the Arcadians' folk history. We have seen that in many places folk history spawned royal oikists or conquerors, but not whole dynasties (most of whose members figured in no remarkable story) for the post-heroic period. There is no discernible reason why the Arcadians should have invented their Cypselid dynasty.

There is, then, some slight evidence that Arcadia was ruled by kings through the Geometric period and into the seventh century.[69] During that time Arcadia was still an *ethnos*, appar-

---

69. Jeffery, *Archaic Greece*, p. 170, takes the last king, Aristocrates, to be "a certainly historical ruler," but supposes that his realm was only Orchomenus. Wade-Gery, *CAH* III, p. 531, regarded the dynasty as reigning over all Arcadia.

ently a pale survivor from the political divisions of the Late Helladic period. Like its northern neighbor Achaea, Arcadia during the Geometric period may have been governed, to the extent that it was governed at all, by institutions quite different from those of the *poleis*.

Messenia   The early history of the Messenian *ethnos* is inordinately complicated.[70] What we have of it was divulged either by the Spartans, who wished to excuse their seizure of Messenia, or by the Messenians themselves after Epaminondas liberated them from Sparta in 370 B.C.

One of the older and more stable elements in the shifting traditions was the tragedy of Cresphontes. As one of the three principal Heraclidae who effected the Return, Cresphontes was a well known figure even before the fifth century. We do not have Euripides' *Cresphontes*,[71] but all extant versions of the myth agree that after the hero had taken over Messenia, he and most of his family were slain.

There are contradictory reports about the assassins. The Spartans claimed that the Messenians themselves had done the deed. In Isocrates' *Archidamus*, an oration composed ca. 366 B.C. in order to uphold Sparta's claim to Messenia in the face of Epaminondas' campaign of liberation, Isocrates has the young Archidamus recount how it was that Sparta had gained control of Messenia in the first place: After Cresphontes had been awarded Messenia, which Heracles had once won from Pylian Neleus, the Messenians wickedly rose in revolt and slew Cresphontes. His sons fled to Sparta and asked for assistance, and the Spartans, "after inquiring of Apollo, and being directed by him to accept this gift and avenge the wronged, thereupon beleaguered the Messenians, and forced them to surrender, and thus gained possession of their territory." Isocrates thus declares that there was one Heraclid king of Messenia,

---

70. Lionel Pearson, "The Pseudo-History of Messenia and its Authors," *Historia* 11 (1962):397–426.

71. Hyginus *Fabulae* 137 and 184 may be based upon the Euripidean play.

Cresphontes.[72] Plato may have believed that the Heraclids kept their throne in Messenia for several generations, but he too regarded them as having been done in by the Messenians, some time before Lycurgus' reform.[73] Both Isocrates and Plato seem to mirror a Spartan tradition that the Spartans took Messenia after (and perhaps because) the Messenians had slain the rightful Heraclid rulers.

The Messenians seem to have told a rather different story, although unfortunately we have it from relatively late sources. Cresphontes, they said, was slain not by the Messenians, but by another Heraclid. And, even more surprisingly, not all of Cresphontes' sons were killed. Let us look at Apollodorus' version of the myth:

Cresphontes had not long reigned over Messene when he was murdered with two of his sons; and Polyphontes, one of the true Heraclids, came to the throne and took to wife, against her will, Merope, the wife of the murdered man. But he too was slain. For Merope had a third son, called Aepytus, whom she gave to her own father to bring up. When he was come to manhood he secretly returned, killed Polyphontes, and recovered the kingdom of his fathers.[74]

Another Messenian version of the myth appears in Pausanias' book on Messenia, and is given in some detail. We are told (Paus. 4.3.6–8) that

the old Messenians were not dispossessed by the Dorians, but agreed to be ruled by Cresphontes and to divide the land with the Dorians. They were induced to give way to them in this by the suspicion which they felt for their rulers, as the Neleidae were originally of Iolcos.

In accord with the amicable relations between the Dorians and the older stock, Cresphontes married Merope, daughter of the Arcadians' King Cypselus, and by her had several children,

---

72. Isocrates *Archidamus* 23 (trans. Norlin). Pearson, "Pseudo-History of Messenia," pp. 404–05, is possibly correct in suggesting that both Isocrates and Plato reckoned with only one generation of Heraclid kingship in Messenia.

73. Plato *Laws* 690D–E.

74. Apollodorus *Bibl.* 2.8.5 (trans. Frazer).

youngest of whom was Aepytus. Cresphontes also decided to move the palace from Pylos, where the Neleids had reigned, to Stenyclerus; and it was there that his descendants kept the palace. Merope sent Aepytus, while an infant, to her father Cypselus (for those who take these things seriously, the Messenian Aepytus is the great-grandson of the Arcadian Aepytus), and so the child escaped when certain nobles slaughtered Cresphontes and the rest of his house. When the child came of age, he returned to Messenia, punished the murderers, recovered the kingdom, and was so esteemed by all his subjects that his descendants were called Aepytidae instead of Heraclidae.

Pausanias is the only ancient author who names the Aepytid kings of Messenia,[75] and he may have learned about them from local traditions. In his fourth book he presents all of the stories attached to early Messenia, treating them all, of course, as serious history. So he told of the dynasty founded by Polycaon and his wife Messene; of the dynasty of Perieres, son of Aeolus and Gorgophone; of Neleus and Nestor; and of other fabled kings who lived before the Return. With the Return there began the last dynasty of Messenian kings:

> Cresphontes
> Aepytus
> Glaucus
> Isthmius
> Dotadas
> Sybotas
> Phintas
> Antiochus and Androcles (joint rulers)
> Euphaes
> Aristodemus (not a son of Euphaes, but an Aepytid)

75. Paus. 4.3.9–10, apparently overlooked by Pearson, "Pseudo-History of Messenia," p. 409: "Pausanias does not give the names of subsequent Heraclid kings of Messenia (nor are they otherwise known) until a quarrel develops with Sparta in the reign of Phintas."

The first four names in the list are apparently mythical,[76] but one cannot readily dismiss the entire line as imaginary. The Aepytid line was not invented, like the Corinthian, for chronographic reasons; nor, like the Temenid, in order to confer Heraclid ancestry on a contemporary king. The myth of the Return did not give rise to the tradition about an Aepytid dynasty. Quite the contrary, the myth of the Return was an extrinsic element, reconciled with the story of the Aepytid dynasty only by the somewhat awkward affiliation of Aepytus to the Heraclid Cresphontes.[77] In an earlier stage of the story, the Aepytids must have been presented not as Dorians at all, but as scions of the pre-Dorian Messenians and Arcadians.

Support for the historicity of the Aepytids is supplied by a lost poem, the *Processional Hymn to the Delian Apollo*, which was probably composed in the late eighth or early seventh century. In describing the reign of Phintas, the seventh king in the Aepytid line, Pausanias says:

In the reign of Phintas, the son of Sybotas, the Messenians for the first time sent an offering and chorus of men to Apollo at Delos. Their processional hymn to the god was composed by Eumelus, this poem being the only one of his that is considered genuine. [4.4.1]

The poem was still available in Pausanias' time, for elsewhere (4.33.2) he quotes two lines from it:

Eumelus, in his processional hymn to Delos, says:
    "For dear to the God of Ithome was the Muse
    whose <lute> is pure and free her sandals."

76. Paus. 4.3.8 mentions another Isthmius, this one a son of Temenus, who helped Aepytus recover his throne. Both Isthmii may have been derived from Poseidon Isthmius.
77. In his notes on fr. 23 of Hellanicus' *Atthis* (*F.Gr.Hist.* no. 323a; p. 52 in the separate volume of notes) Jacoby made the generalization that when a tradition affiliates a family's eponymous hero to a "real" founder, we usually have "proof of the genuine pedigree having been manipulated."

I think that he wrote the lines because he knew that they held a musical contest.[78]

It is not certain, of course, that Eumelus was the author of the poem. Nor do we know whether the hymn named Phintas or any other Messenian king, although that possibility must remain open. At the very least, however, Pausanias found that the poem fit in with the tradition that the Messenians were still ruled by monarchs in Eumelus' time.

What were the Messenians doing at the sanctuary of Delian Apollo, an eminently Ionian shrine? One suspects that ca. 700 B.C. the Messenians did not yet describe themselves as Dorian, or their kings as descendants of Heracles. There is reason to believe, let us conclude, that during the Geometric period the Messenian *ethnos* was ruled by kings who traced their descent to the hero Aepytus, whose famous tomb lay in Arcadia.

Lacedaemon   It is customary to refer to the Agiads and Eurypontids of Classical Sparta as "kings," despite the fact that they lived in ordinary houses, wore no regalia, and struck the Eastern barbarians as thoroughly common.[79] The traditional classification rests on two considerations: the Spartan leaders' title was *basileus* and their position was hereditary and, therefore, lifelong.

We are finding, however, that the semantic fields of the English word "king" and the Greek word *basileus* are not at all identical. Various magistrates in the Greek republics bore the title *basileus*. Some of these officials had an annual term, some may have held a tenured position. In Sparta we find *basileis* who hold their office for life, but that does not by itself make kings of them.

A more important question is whether the Spartan *basileus* ruled the state. Obviously he did not. That he had to share his office with a colleague was merely one circumstance that distinguished him from kings as we know them in other ages and

78. Eumelus, fr. 13 (Kinkel).
79. For the Egyptians' reaction to Agesilaus see Plutarch *Agesilaus* 36.

nations. Even together, the two *basileis* no more ruled Sparta than the two consuls ruled Rome or the two suffetes ruled Carthage (the suffetes too are sometimes called *basileis* in our Greek sources; but because they served an annual term few historians have succumbed to the temptation to bestow upon them the English title "kings"). Instead, the Spartan *basileis* carried out the decisions of the gerousia and apella, decisions which of course they had helped to make. Let us recall Xenophon's account of the powers that Lycurgus assigned to the *basileis*: "He arranged that the *basileus* perform all the public sacrifices on behalf of the polis, on the grounds that the *basileus* was descended from a god; and that he lead the army wherever the polis might send it" (*Lac. Pol.* 15.2). To this we can add that the *basileis* notarized adoptions, judged suits that involved heiresses or public roads, and selected citizens to serve as *proxenoi* for other states.[80] These constitute an impressive set of responsibilities; but they do not set the Spartan *basileus* significantly apart from republican magistrates, or distinguish the *basileia* from an *archē hypeuthynos*.[81]

Relevant to this point is the relationship of the *basileis* to the ephors. After remarking that the *basileis* had many privileges (they received a double portion of food at the common meals; they were given one piglet from every sow's litter; and near their homes the state maintained a fresh-water pond), Xenophon goes on to say:

And for a *basileus* all rise from their seats, except that the ephors do not rise from their ephoric benches. And every month they exchange oaths with each other, the ephors on behalf of the polis, the *basileus* on his own behalf. For the *basileus*, the oath is that he will conduct his office (βασιλεύσειν) according to the established laws of the polis; for the polis, the oath is that it will see to it that, if the *basileus* abides by his oath, his *basileia* will be free of vexations.[82] [*Lac. Pol.* 15.6–7]

80. On the duties of the *basileis* see Busolt, *Staatskunde* 1:673–78.
81. See p. 35, n. 62.
82. ἀστυφέλικτον τὴν βασιλείαν παρέξειν does not mean, as E. C. Marchant translates it in the Loeb edition of the *Lac. Pol.*, "keep the kingship un-

Each of the *basileis*, even while leading the army on campaign, was accompanied by two ephors who played the part of official watchdogs.[83] More surprisingly, on a clear night every ninth year the ephors watched the sky for a shooting star; the celestial sign would indicate that the gods were displeased with one of the *basileis*.[84] When a *basileus* did go on trial, as happened at least seven times in the fifth century, his jury consisted of the other twenty-nine members of the gerousia and the five ephors.[85]

In fact, supervision ("it is certain that, as their name implies, the ephors were supervisors, wardens")[86] of the *basileis* may have been the reason for the establishment of the ephorate. It is often assumed that the Spartan ephors supervised the helots, or possibly the social system, but the other states which had ephors had neither helots nor an unusual social system: Thera and her colonial offspring, Cyrene and Euhesperides, Lucanian Heraclea and, since Heraclea was a Tarentine colony, presumably Tarentum itself.[87] We have already encountered

shaken." That translation implies that the ephors will ward off possible assassins, constitutional reformers, or something equally dire. Apparently *stypheligmos* was not so serious as all that; Aristophanes (*Eq.* 537) uses the word in the sense of "abuse" or "harassment."

83. Xenophon *Lac. Pol.* 13.5. For their characterization see D. M. Lewis, *Sparta and Persia* (Leiden: Brill, 1977), p. 44: "Unlike Athenian strategoi, Spartan kings have official watchdogs permanently with them."

84. Plutarch *Agis.* 11.

85. Although most historians tend to look at the *basileis* as less powerful than the gerousia or the ephors, some have tried to reverse the picture. See, for example, Paul Cloché, "Sur la rôle des rois de Sparte," *LEC* 17 (1949): pp. 113–38; G. E. M. de Sainte Croix, *The Origins of the Peloponnesian War* (London: Duckworth, 1972), pp. 138–49; and C. G. Thomas, "On the Role of the Spartan Kings," *Historia* 23 (1974):257–70. For an argument to the contrary see Lewis, *Sparta and Persia*, pp. 43–44. Lewis lists the fifth-century occasions on which a *basileus* was brought to trial and, more often than not, stripped of his office.

86. Pavel Oliva, *Sparta and her Social Problems* [Amsterdam (Hakkert), and Prague (Academia), 1971], p. 126. Busolt, *Staatskunde*, 1:684, translates the term as "Aufseher."

87. Busolt, *Staatskunde* 1, pp. 683–84, n. 2. The evidence for ephors in Thera comes from inscriptions of the Hellenistic and Roman periods: *IG* XII, part 3, nos. 322, 326, 330, and 336. For Cyrene see *SEG* IX, no. 1 (line 33), and

Aristophilides, *basileus* in Tarentum at the end of the sixth century, and we shall see that there were hereditary *basileis* in Archaic Thera and Cyrene. It is probably not a coincidence that most of the states in which ephors are indicated are also states that are known to have had a hereditary *basileia*. Whether or not the ephorate and the hereditary *basileia* were intended to be complementary, the Spartan *basileia* appears to have been very much an *arche hypeuthynos*.

The double *basileia* as we know it is completely integrated with the ephorate and the gerousia, and it is difficult to imagine it functioning without these other components of the *eunomia*. Is it conceivable that before the *eunomia* was established, or, as Herodotus would say, before Lycurgus instituted the gerousia and ephorate, Sparta was ruled by two kings, each having sovereign power over the state? We have all heard about kingdoms divided between two princes, or about co-regencies of father and son, but one can hardly visualize a single state ruled by two sovereigns.

I have argued in detail elsewhere that it is likely that around the middle of the eighth century the Spartans instituted their *eunomia*, that the double *basileia* was one of the innovations of that time, and that the model for the new regime was furnished by the Phoenicians.[88] Here it will be enough to recall that the list of Sparta's Eurypontid *basileis* is noticeably unstable and defective in its early entries. Although at various times Lycurgus was claimed for both houses, there was apparent agreement that the first Eurypontid *basileus* in the new *eunomia* was Charillus, usually identified as the nephew and

the statement in Heraclides' synopsis of Aristotle's *Politeiai*, no. 18 in the edition of M. R. Dilts, *Heraclidis Lembi Excerpta Politiarum* (*GRBS*, Monograph no. 5, 1971). Ephors at Euhesperides are mentioned in an inscription of ca. 350 B.C.: P. M. Fraser, *Gnomon* 29 (1957): p. 18, n. 1. On the ephorate at Heraclea see *IG* XIV, no. 645. There were also ephors in the various free Laconian towns of the Roman period, and in Messenia after 370 B.C., but both can only be late innovations. See George Huxley, *Early Sparta* (London: Faber and Faber, 1962), pp. 115–16, n. 229.

88. Drews, "Phoenicians, Carthage and the Spartan *Eunomia*," *AJP* 100 (TEKMHRION. *A Special Issue in Honor of James Henry Oliver.* 1979), pp. 45–58.

ward of Lycurgus.[89] Between Eurypon and Charillus (ca. 750 B.C.?) there are only two or three names in the lists:

Herodotus 8.131	Pausanias 3.7	Plutarch Lyc. 1
Eurypon	Eurypon	Eurypon
Prytanis	Prytanis	Eunomus
Polydectes	Eunomus	Polydectes
Eunomus	Polydectes	Charillus
Charillus	Charillus	

Eurypon is the eponymous hero of the house, and Prytanis and Eunomus are personifications. It is probable that Charillus, perhaps the son of Polydectes, was the first historical *basileus* in the Eurypontid line.[90]

The Agiad list (Herodotus 6.51 says that the Agiad house was the older and more honored of the two) appears more stable and solid. It is no longer than the Eurypontid list, with only sixteen entries between the Return and the Persian Wars, but its early

89. Our earliest witness, Simonides, regarded Lycurgus as the son of Prytanis (Plut. *Lyc.* 1), and presumably as the uncle of Charillus. Plutarch says that "all the rest" of his authorities presented the following genealogy:

Eurypon

Eunomus

Polydectes   Lycurgus

Charillus

Among those who presented Lycurgus as Charillus' uncle was Aristotle (*Pol.* 1271b). Herodotus alone makes Lycurgus an Agiad (1.65.4 where Lycurgus is uncle of Leobotes).

90. That Charillus was the first Eurypontid *basileus* has been suggested before. See K. M. T. Chrimes, *Ancient Sparta* (New York: Philosophical Library, 1952), pp. 337–38. Although James Oliver did not suggest a date for the first Eurypontid *basileus*, his reconstruction of the development is similar to that given above: "The Agiads were the royal house at an early period when there was only one royal house. The power of the Agiads was subsequently limited by the aristocrats, who elevated a prytanis from their own ranks and obtained for him a position of parity as a second ruler." Oliver, *Demokratia, the Gods and the Free World* (Baltimore: Johns Hopkins Univ. Press, 1960), p. 7.

entries are reasonable enough to suggest that there may well have been Agiad leaders before the eighth century, and before the establishment of the *eunomia*. Could these Agiads have been kings? We have seen that there is some evidence for kings in Achaea, Arcadia, and Messenia in the Geometric period, and it is possible that the Agiads were kings of the same kind. Achaea, Arcadia, and Messenia were ancient *ethnē*, quite unlike *poleis* such as Miletus and Ephesus, Corinth and Chalcis. As the Catalogue of Ships suggests,[91] Arcadia and Messenia may have been fairly centralized in the Late Helladic period; but during the Dark Age they must have tended toward that same fragmentation to which the Argolid and Boeotia fell victim. It is possible that what unity they maintained in the Geometric period was furnished by their Cypselid and Aepytid monarchies.

There are several indications that in the Dark Age the Agiads were weak kings of a large and disintegrating *ethnos*. We recall that Cleomenes claimed that he was not a Dorian but an Achaean. The Herodotean story (5.72) assumes that the Greeks had at least heard about an Agiad claim to a lineage that went back beyond the Return, to the pre-Dorian "Achaeans." That the Spartans' state preserved the contours of a pre-Dorian *ethnos* is clear from the name of their state: although we call it "Sparta," the Spartans themselves always referred to it as "Lacedaemon."[92] In the Submycenaean period Lacedaemon included, the Catalogue of Ships indicates,[93] seven towns in the Eurotas valley and the coastal plain of Laconia. Throughout the Archaic and Classical periods "Lacedaemon" regularly stood for the entire district of Laconia, and it is exceptional to find it as a synonym for the town of Sparta. On the other hand, "Sparta" invariably stands for the town (the single passage in which it stands for all Laconia must be, Victor Ehrenberg de-

91. *Iliad* 2.591–602, 603–14.
92. For a comprehensive presentation of the usage of the terms "Lacedaemon," "Sparta," and "Spartiate," see A. von Lippold, s.v. Sparta, *RE* III², 1267–80.
93. *Iliad* 2.581–90.

cided, an "unrichtiger Sprachgebrauch"[94]). It would appear that through the Dark Age there persisted a vague unity of all Lacedaemon.[95] This unity would have been more nominal than actual, since in the eighth century Sparta apparently had to coerce some of the non-Dorian towns of Lacedaemon to accept her regime. I would suggest, therefore, that during the Dark Age there continued to be kings of Lacedaemon, just as there seem to have been kings of Achaea, Arcadia, and Messenia. In Mycenaean times the *wanax* of Lacedaemon is thought to have ruled from the natural citadel known as Therapnae, three kilometers to the southeast of Sparta, and on the opposite, eastern bank of the Eurotas.[96] The citadel of Therapnae was abandoned at the end of the Late Helladic III B period. Late in the eighth century, however, perhaps stimulated by the circulation of the *Iliad*, the Spartans built atop Therapnae a shrine to Menelaus.[97] Where the Agiads might have lived during the Dark Age, and whether they were "Achaean" or Dorian, must remain open questions. At any rate, they could have had little power. The various Spartan legends concerning Lycurgus and the *eunomia* assume that before Lycurgus' time Lacedaemon was ruled by kings, but the legends do not suggest that the *eunomia* was instituted because the kings had been despotic or even autocratic. To the contrary, the traditions implied that there had been too little control, too much stasis and anarchy, and that Lycurgus' re-

94. V. Ehrenberg, "Spartiaten und Lakedaimonier," *Hermes* 59 (1924), p. 43, n. 2.

95. Almost nothing can be said about the Submycenaean period; see Vincent Desborough, *The Greek Dark Ages* (New York: St. Martin's, 1972), p. 332. In the Protogeometric period, however, Laconian pottery follows a single style; see Paul Cartledge, *Sparta and Lakonia. A Regional History 1300–362 BC* (London: Routledge and Kegan Paul, 1979), p. 83.

96. On recent work at Therapnae see H. W. Catling, "Excavations at the Menelaion, Sparta, 1973–1976," in *Arch. Rep. for 1976–77* no. 23, pp. 24–42.

97. Catling, "Menelaion," p. 34. J. N. Coldstream, "Hero-Cults in the Age of Homer," *JHS* 96 (1976): 8–17 argues persuasively that the explosion of hero-cults in the late eighth century was the result of the circulation of the *Iliad*.

form brought order out of chaos.[98] The reform of ca. 750 B.C., which enabled the polis of Sparta to establish control over the entire *ethnos* of Lacedaemon, probably abolished a weak and ineffectual Lacedaemonian monarchy and put in its place a well organized oligarchical regime, in which the reigning Agiad king of Lacedaemon and a Eurypontid "kinsman" were made *basileis*.

One last point to be made is that if there was, as seems probable, a king of Lacedaemon before the institution of the *eunomia*, there is no reason to assume that his title was *basileus*. In the following chapter we shall see that in the Dark Age the Greek word that came closest to the semantic field of the English word "king" was not *basileus*. For the Agiad and Eurypontid officials in the *eunomia* the conventional, if not the original, title was certainly *basileus*. The Great Rhetra and its rider referred to the two officials as *archagetai*, but as early as the middle of the seventh century Tyrtaeus was calling them *basileis*.[99] In the fifth century, of course, they were invariably called *basileis*.

CENTRAL GREECE

The heterogeneous states of central Greece did not have a share in the myth of the Return. Aegina was thought to have become a Dorian state long after the Return. Athens and Euboea escaped the invasion, and Boeotia was said to have been taken by the Boeotians, who came from Arne in Thessaly, sixty years after the fall of Troy. We must treat separately the traditions of each of the states in central Greece.

98. Herodotus (1.65.2) says that before Lycurgus' reform the Lacedaemonians were *kakonomotatoi*, and could not get along either with each other or with anybody else. Thucydides (1.18.1) had the same opinion: "Of all the states we know, Lacedaemon, after the settlement of the Dorians who now inhabit the land, was in stasis for the longest time."

99. For the Rhetra and its rider see Plutarch *Lycurgus* 6. For the term *basileis* see Tyrtaeus 3.3 and 4.1 (Diehl). On the parallels between the Spartan *basileis* and the Carthaginian *basileis* ("suffetes") see Drews, "Phoenicians," pp. 53–57.

Aegina   The Aeginetans did not have a heroic dynasty. One Thessalian figure whom they appropriated was Aeacus, father of Peleus and grandfather of Achilles and Ajax. Homer (*Il.* 21.189) had called Aeacus a son of Zeus, but had not identified Aeacus' mother. In the Archaic period it was discovered that the mother was Aegina,[1] and thus the Aeginetans acquired Aeacus as their heroic king. No line of kings came with Aeacus. His famous sons, Peleus and Telamon, had gone off to rule Phthiotic Achaea and Salamis, and it was said by some that the Phocians had received their name from a third son, Phocus. There was no Aeacid left to rule Aegina, and the Aeginetans invented none. Our conclusion has been stated concisely by Pausanias: "They can mention no king of the island except Aeacus" (2.29.2).

Athens   It is not improbable that from a palace on the Athenian Acropolis, during the Late Helladic period, a series of kings ruled all of Attica, a vast area roughly the size of *ethnē* such as Arcadia and Messenia. It is even possible that Theseus and Codrus were historical figures, ruling during the Mycenaean and Submycenaean periods. But whether there still were kings on the Acropolis in the Geometric period is quite another question. The only evidence for kings at so late a date is the Athenian kinglist which details two very unequal dynasties. The first dynasty, as given by chronographers from the author of the Parian Marble to Eusebius, consisted of fifteen storied kings. It began with Cecrops and ended, two generations after the Trojan War, with Thymoetes, the coward who gave up his throne rather than face the Boeotian king, Xanthus, in single combat. In Thymoetes' place there stepped forward

---

1. She was, the scholiast at *Iliad* 21.186 says, the daughter of Asopus. Since several rivers bore the name Asopus, the eponymous heroine of many a polis was identified as Asopus' daughter. In addition to a list affiliated to the Boeotian Asopus, there was a list of the daughters of the little Asopus near Sicyon. The latter list seems to have been worked out by Eumelus. See C. M. Bowra, "The Daughters of Asopus," *Problems in Greek Poetry* (Oxford: Clarendon, 1953), pp. 57–58.

Melanthus, freshly arrived from Pylos. The second dynasty of
Athenian kings, that of Melanthus, Codrus, and their less famous successors, was also made up of fifteen kings. Let us
recall who they were and how many years they reigned:[2]

Melanthus	37
Codrus	21
Medon	20
Acastus	36
Archippus	19
Thersippus	41
Phorbas	31
Megacles	30
Diognetus	28
Pherecles	19
Ariphron	20
Thespieus	27
Agamestor	20
Aeschylus	23
Alcmaeon	2

In the Year of Abraham 1263 (753/2 B.C.) the Athenians replaced their kings with archons who ruled each for ten years.
Eusebius lists seven decennial archons:

Charops
Aesimides
Clidicus
Hippomenes
Leocrates
Apsander
Eryxias

At this point (683/2 B.C.) the Athenians established the annual
archonship, Creon being the first to hold that position.

The list of Athenian kings and decennial archons was of

2. The Eusebian list is given at *Chron.* I, 181–90 (Schoene). Eusebius
claims Castor of Rhodes as his immediate source.

course taken seriously through the Renaissance and the seventeenth century. But scholars have dealt harshly with the list. In 1846 George Grote duly presented the list, but then remarked:

Such is the series of names by which we step down from the level of legend to that of history. . . . Above 683 B.C. the Attic antiquaries have provided us with a string of names, which we must take as we find them, without being able to warrant the whole or to separate the false from the true. There is no reason to doubt the general fact that Athens, *like so many other communities of Greece*, was in its primitive time governed by an hereditary line of kings [my italics].[3]

William Smith discounted the whole sequence, from Cecrops to the last decennial archon, as a "legendary account."[4] But late in the nineteenth century critical scholars were brought sharply to heel, and the list was treated with unaccustomed respect. This about-face was executed in part because by that time Schliemann's excavations had given the Greek myths a new respectability, and in part because of the discovery, in 1890, of the *Athenaion Politeia*. The papyrus indicated that already in the fourth century the main lines of the list had been known, and had been accepted by no less an authority than Aristotle. More than that, it showed (*Ath. Pol.* 3) that one of the figures in the list—Acastus—was featured in the oath which fourth-century archons took when they entered office. The list had not, it seemed, been fabricated by "Attic antiquaries" after all. In what now seems a curious twist, Eduard Meyer dismissed Codrus and all his predecessors as inventions because the stories told about them showed them to be figures of oral tradition, but accepted at face value Codrus' successors ("die Reihe der thatenlosen historischen Könige") because no traditions were attached to them.[5] Their names, he believed, had been preserved on written documents from the eighth century to Aristotle's time. Meyer also accepted the list of seven decennial archons for the years 753–683 B.C. Wilamowitz was

3. Grote, *History of Greece*, 2:269.
4. William Smith, *History of Greece* (Boston: Jenks, Hickling and Swan, 1854), p. 89. Smith is best known for his dictionary of classical antiquity.
5. Meyer, *Geschichte des Alterthums*, 2:347–48.

even more insistent on the value of the chronographers' list. In an 1898 article on the Codrid kings, Wilamowitz declared that there could be no serious doubts about the soundness of the list, and he supposed that the keeping of written records in Athens had begun ca. 750 B.C.[6]

Scepticism, however, continued. In 1904 Otto Seeck concluded that, despite the evidence of the *Athenaion Politeia*, the second dynasty of kings and decennial archons was a fabrication. He proposed that it was concocted by a historian, perhaps Charon of Lampsacus, who needed to bridge the gap between the supposed date for Codrus, or Medon, and the beginning of the list of annual archons: the historian built his bridge by transforming the first twenty or so annual archons, on the list that he had received, into kings and decennial archons.[7] Max Cary found that "the lists of the kings are so full of flaws that the only safe course is to accept none of their data except where they are confirmed by independent evidence." The creator of the list, Cary noted, surely wrote after Herodotus, "for Herodotus knew the names of only four kings, whereas the lists enumerate thirty."[8]

Felix Jacoby, in a series of studies spanning fifty years, made by far the most important contribution to an understanding of the Athenian kinglist.[9] What Jacoby concluded, essentially, was that the entire list was constructed by Hellanicus, late in

6. Ulrich von Wilamowitz-Moellendorff, "Die lebenslänglichen Archonten Athens," *Hermes* 33 (1898):125: "Es kann doch niemand im Ernst an sich für unwahrscheinlich halten, dass eine solche offizielle Aufzeichnung um 750 in Athen begonnen ist."

7. Otto Seeck, "Quellenstudien zu des Aristoteles Verfassungsgeschichte Athens," *Klio* 4 (1904):292–306. Seeck supposed that Acastus, because he appeared in the oath, was the first annual archon.

8. "Early Athens," *CAH* III, pp. 586–87.

9. Jacoby first addressed the matter in "Die attische Königsliste," *Klio* 2 (1902):406–39; his last and best discussion of it is to be found in the two supplementary volumes of the *Fragmente der griechischen Historiker*. In the first of these volumes, subtitled *A Commentary on the Ancient Historians of Athens* (Leiden: Brill, 1954), pp. 43–51 are devoted to fr. 23 of Hellanicus' history of Athens. The footnotes for this commentary on fr. 23 occupy sixteen pages of small print (pp. 49–65) in the accompanying volume of notes.

the fifth century, and was modified only slightly by atthidographers in the fourth century and chronographers in the third. Hellanicus assembled his heroic first dynasty from the traditions, oral and written, about the heroic past. The names that followed Codrus, far from being copied by Hellanicus from an old document, were Hellanicus' own deductions (for example, from the oath of the nine archons) and surmises. Their function was to fill the lacuna between the heroic past and the first entry on the Athenians' list of annual archons. Whereas Wilamowitz could not imagine anybody doubting the historicity of Codrus' successors, nobody who has read Jacoby's analysis is likely to regard the list as having any historical value except as an illustration of the way that an ancient scholar might deal with the distant past. Let me quote here Jacoby's summary statement:

There seems to me to be no doubt of H. [Hellanicus] having constructed the pedigree of the Melanthidai as he did that of the Erechtheidai, and in the same manner, with the only difference that he had much less traditional material at his disposal for the second list: the earlier kings almost without exception occurred in single stories and they had only to be brought into a sequence and fitted into Panhellenic chronology; of the Medontidai however Hippomenes seems to have been the only one to whom a story was attached. There was an empty space between the two dates, fixed for H. for several reasons, of the Ionian migration and the first annual archon, and this he evidently filled with a series of Athenian names of distinguished sound. The list handed down to us . . . seems to me perfectly intelligible as a construction built from names occurring in the great *genê* of the sixth and fifth centuries.[10]

Although the atthidographers and chronographers took over Hellanicus' list, certain changes in it had to be made. The list originally must have contained at least ten decennial archons, for the Parian Marble placed the last lifetime ruler, Aeschylus, at least thirty years earlier than Castor and Eusebius placed him. It was probably Eratosthenes, needing to fit the Athenian

10. Jacoby, *Commentary*, 1:51.

rulers into his own panhellenic chronology, who dropped three of the decennial archons. The original list, again reflected in the Parian Marble, seems to have presented Medon and his successors as kings; but in order to accommodate a tradition that Codrus had been the last king, Codrus' successors were retitled "archons for life," perhaps by the atthidographer Cleidemus.[11]

The consideration that tells most against the validity of the second dynasty is not the presence in the list of Alcmaeonid and Philaid names such as Alcmaeon, Megacles, and Agamestor, or of an Ariphron (the name of Pericles' grandfather). Nor is it that there is no evidence for written kinglists of any kind in Greece before the fifth century. What is decisive is that the names that follow Codrus are nothing more than names. They figure in no historical accounts, in no anecdotes, not even in aetiology. There are no traditions about them, and one may conclude that they are chronographic fillers because they appear only in chronographic contexts. Aside from Eusebius' *Chronicle* there is only one place where we meet Eryxias, listed as the last decennial archon: Velleius Paterculus (1.8) says that "ex iis qui denis annis praefuerunt, primus fuit Charops, ultimus Eryxias," and this statement too is strictly chronographic. Eryxias' predecessor, Apsander, appears only in Eusebius' *Chronicle*, as do Leocrates and Clidicus. The second decennial archon, Aesimides, does make one appearance outside the *Chronicle:* in Pausanias 4.5.10. About to narrate the great war that Sparta and Messenia fought, Pausanias, affecting Thucydidean precision, stops to pinpoint chronologically the Spartan attack on Ampheia, which started the war. This attack, says Pausanias, occurred in the second year of the ninth Olympiad:

In Athens there were not as yet archons appointed annually by lot; for at first the people deprived the descendants of Melanthus, called Medontidae, of most of their power, transforming the kingship into a

---

11. Jacoby, *Commentary,* 1:46–48; on the high chronology of the Parian Marble see Jacoby's commentary on *F.Gr.Hist.* no. 239.

constitutional office; afterwards they limited their tenure of office to ten years. At the time of the seizure of Ampheia, Aesimides the son of Aeschylus was holding his fifth year of office at Athens.

Like Velleius' reference to Eryxias, this solitary reference to Aesimides is chronographic. So also are the two references to the first decennial archon, Charops: in addition to the passage from Velleius quoted above, Charops is mentioned by Dionysius of Halicarnassus (*Ant. Rom.* 1.71.5, 75.3) in order to fix the date of the foundation of Rome. (Romulus and Remus founded Rome when Charops was in the first year of his ten-year term.) The *only* decennial archon about whom there was a story in antiquity was Hippomenes. Hippomenes began his career in story as a cruel father who, upon discovering his daughter and her lover in an illicit relationship, killed the lover and confined the daughter and a horse in an enclosure, where the horse killed the girl. (Hippomenes' name perhaps grew out of ἱππομανές a plant supposed to make horses go mad.) This dark affair occurred in an area of Athens known ever after as "Place of the Horse and Girl." In an early version of the story, Hippomenes is simply identified as "a citizen."[12] All agreed that he had lived a very long time ago. This aetiological figure was, if we may use the oxymoron, the only "truly mythical" person to be listed among the decennial archons. In the list, and in the atthidographers' histories, he was presented as the fourth decennial archon and as the last descendant of Melanthus to hold that position, his successors being chosen from the general Athenian nobility. As Jacoby says, "the story of Hippomenes . . . is a typical aition because surely it had originally no other purpose but to explain the name Παρ' ἵππον καὶ κόρην of a locality. But the *Atthis* made Hippomenes a Medontid, and made the disappearance of the second family of kings the consequence of his gruesome deed."[13]

If the Classical Athenians knew no stories about the decennial archons (Hippomenes excepted), whom the list dates to the period 753–683 B.C., it will be no surprise to find that

---

12. Aeschines *In Timarch.* 182: ἀνὴρ εἷς τῶν πολιτῶν.
13. Jacoby, *Atthis*, p. 145.

neither had they heard anything about the Melanthid kings who preceded the decennial archons. Aeschylus, whose twenty-three-year reign should have been remembered for something, appears only in the Pausanias passage on Ampheia quoted above (Paus. 4.5.10), on the Parian Marble, and in Eusebius' *Chronicle*. Aeschylus' father and grandfather, Agamestor and Thespieus, fared even worse, being mentioned only by Eusebius. Such is also the case for Thespieus' father and predecessor, Ariphron, nor do we find any other Melanthid king outside the chronographic tradition until we work our way back to the solid ground of truly mythical figures at the head of the list.

In summary, before Hellanicus wrote his history of Athens, the Athenians told stories about kings before, during, and shortly after the Trojan War. The last of the storied kings was Codrus, whose sons went off to Ionia to found cities. What happened after Codrus was not clear: some fifth-century Athenians may have thought that Codrus' descendants ruled as kings, others thought that after Codrus the king was replaced by an archon.[14] During the 420s B.C., and so too late for Herodotus to consult, an archonlist was set up in the Athenian agora. Archons from as early as the beginning of the sixth century are listed on the recovered fragments, and it is likely that the inscription began with Creon, in 682 B.C.[15] Once the list was set up, historians could refer to it, as Hellanicus did. But historians were also prompted, since the list did not after all run back to Codrus, to explain who had been in control between the time of the heroic kings and Creon's archonship. And this too Hellanicus did. His list shows us only how a scholar of the late fifth century went about reconstructing the post-heroic past. There may have been kings of Attica in the

14. See Jacoby, *Commentary*, 1:48: "The story of Kodros may originally have been a simple aition which, being connected with a Peloponnesian war, gave the answer to the question why Athens was not ruled by kings like Sparta."

15. For the fragments see Meiggs and Lewis, *Greek Historical Inscriptions*, no. 6.

Late Helladic period, but the last remembered king was
Codrus.

Eretria and Chalcis   These two cities were among the most
important eighth-century *poleis.* Eretria was built ca. 800 B.C.,
probably by settlers from the nearby site for which we have
only a modern name, Lefkandi.[16] The Euboeans seem to have
taken the lead, late in the ninth century, in establishing an
emporium at Al Mina on the Orontes, and it was they who
took the first steps in colonizing the west.[17] The settlement on
Pithecusae, in the Bay of Naples, was a joint entreprise of the
Chalcidians and Eretrians. Established ca. 775 B.C., it was
intended to serve as a metalworking center, receiving ores
from Elba and perhaps from the Etruscan coast.[18] In the middle
of the eighth century Chalcis and Eretria, joined by Euboeic
Cyme, founded Italian Cumae, and in the second half of the
eighth century the Euboeans began to set up colonies in Sicily.
Since Eretria and Chalcis were the earliest Greek *poleis* to
distinguish themselves, one is especially curious about their
early form of government.

Very little has come down to us on the subject. But it is quite
clear that no kings of Chalcis or Eretria were associated with
the colonial projects. In fact, no ancient author says anything
about a king of either polis (the *Certamen Homeri et Hesiodi,*
as noted in the introductory chapter, calls Hesiod's Amphidamas "king of Euboea," but Hesiod himself made no such
egregious mistake). At *Politics* 1289b, to support his generalization that the government of a polis is determined by the

16. Paul Auberson and Karl Schefold, *Führer durch Eretria* (Bern: Francke,
1972), p. 19.
17. John Boardman, *The Greeks Overseas* (Baltimore: Penguin, 1964), pp.
63–65, first demonstrated the Euboeans' responsibility for the Al Mina emporium and showed the significance of the enterprise. On the Chalcidians and
Eretrians in the west see David Ridgway, "The First Western Greeks: Campa-
nian Coasts and Southern Etruria," *Greeks, Celts and Romans: Studies in
Venture and Resistance,* ed. Christopher and Sonia Hawkes (Towota, N.J.:
Rowman and Littlefield, 1973), pp. 5–38.
18. Jeffery Klein, "A Greek Metalworking Quarter. Eighth Century Excavations on Ischia," *Expedition* 14 (1972):34–39.

people who defend it, Aristotle remarks that ἐπὶ τῶν ἀρχαίων χρόνων the Chalcidians and Eretrians had oligarchical regimes, because those peoples' battles were fought by their cavalrymen (hippeis). "Ancient times" seem to have lasted until late in the sixth century, for ca. 506 B.C. the Athenians defeated the Chalcidians and took over much of the land that belonged to the Hippobotae of Chalcis. "The Hippobotae," Herodotus explains (5.77.2), "are what the wealthy Chalcidians are called." As far as later Greeks knew, the oligarchical regimes were already functioning in the eighth century. After Strabo had recited the Eretrians' and Chalcidians' colonial foundations at Cumae and in Sicily he noted,

these colonies were sent out, as Aristotle says, when the politeia of the so-called Hippobotae was in control. At the head of this were men who, on the basis of wealth, ruled aristocratically.[19] [10.1.8]

A few paragraphs further on Strabo furnishes a more detailed impression of Archaic Euboea, taking his information (10.1.10) from an inscription on a column in the temple of Artemis Amarynthia. The inscription specified that the Eretrians' procession to the temple consisted of three thousand hoplites, six hundred cavalrymen, and sixty chariots. Eighth-century Eretria, or Chalcis, was probably smaller. But even in the eighth century the two cities seem to have been relatively large and wealthy, and each was apparently ruled by an oligarchy based on wealth.

Thebes   Our survey will close with Thebes, a state which claimed no kings who concern us. After the heroic reigns of Oedipus, Eteocles, and Creon, the Thebans fell on evil days. The last king with whom they were credited, and then only by courtesy of the Athenians, was Xanthus, who was gulled by Melanthus in their single combat (even Xanthus is identified as king not of Thebes, but of Boeotia).[20] After Xanthus' death, says Pausanias in his description of Boeotia (9.5.16), the

---

19. The Aristotle whom Strabo quotes may have been a fourth-century historian, Aristotle of Chalcis; but, as Jacoby suggests in his commentary on that historian (F.Gr.Hist. no. 423), it was more likely the Stagirite.

20. Hellanicus (F.Gr.Hist. no. 323a), fr. 23.

Thebans chose "to have a government of several people" (διὰ πλειόνων πολιτεύεσθαι) rather than to be ruled by a monarch. When the Persians invaded Greece in 480 B.C., the Thebans were still ruled by "a *dynasteia* of a few men" (Thucydides 3.62.3), and the city did not contrive a proper *politeia* (an oligarchy, as it happened) until the middle of the fifth century.

CONCLUSION

The results of our survey can now be tabulated. Several *ethnē*, all in the Peloponnese, may have been ruled by kings through the Geometric period: Achaea, Arcadia, Messenia and, until it was reconstituted ca. 750 B.C., Lacedaemon. Our sources do not indicate, on the other hand, that those states which are recognizable as *poleis* were ruled by kings in the Geometric period. Of the *poleis* reviewed here, for only three were post-heroic dynasties claimed. The other *poleis* can be divided into three categories: (a) those for which heroic kings are explicitly denied, (b) those for which no post-heroic king is mentioned, and (c) those for which the evidence is superficially equivocal. Here is a list of the various *poleis* in the appropriate categories:

Post-heroic dynasty claimed	Post-heroic kings denied	Post-heroic kings not mentioned	Evidence superficially equivocal
Corinth	Miletus	Ephesus	Chios
Argos	Sicyon	Erythrae	Samos
Athens	Megara	Colophon	Cyme
	Aegina	Phocaea	Tarentum
	Thebes	Teos	Syracuse
		Myus	
		Clazomenae	
		Lebedos	
		Priene	
		Smyrna	
		Mytilene	
		Chalcis	
		Eretria	

For each of the five *poleis* in the last column, analysis readily disproves the putative evidence for post-heroic kings. Aristophilides of Tarentum, who delivered Democedes from the Persians, must not have been a monarch but a republican *basileus;* the same is true for Amphicrates of Samos and, if they ever existed, for Agamemnon of Cyme and Hippoclus of Chios; Pollis was neither a monarch of Syracuse nor a republican *basileus,* but an aetiological invention. We may conclude, therefore, that for only three of the twenty-six *poleis* reviewed do the ancient sources indicate a post-heroic monarchy.

Finally, the evidence (in each case a kinglist) which attributes a post-heroic dynasty to Argos, Corinth, and Athens is factitious. The Corinthian list was assembled by several writers, from Ephorus to a post-Apollodoran chronographer, in order to bridge the gap between the Return and Cypselus' coup. The several Argive lists were created by Theopompus and later historians in order to demonstrate Philip's Heraclid ancestry. Hellanicus produced the Athenian list toward the end of the fifth century, in order to fill the void between Melanthus and Codrus on the far side and the recently erected archonlist on the near side. There is no credible evidence for kings in the *poleis* of Geometric Greece.

CHAPTER III   THE MEANING OF *BASILEUS* IN GEOMETRIC AND ARCHAIC GREECE

Many students of early Greek history and literature believe that the background against which the Homeric stories unfold is by and large a reflection of Protogeometric and Geometric Greece. The stories themselves are often regarded as having originated in Mycenaean Greece, but the manners and morals as well as the institutions of the heroes are held to be coloration from the tenth and ninth centuries, especially on the Ionian side of the Aegean. Though still popular, this assumption originated before there was any archaeological evidence on Greek prehistory and can be found in the classic histories of George Grote and Adolf Holm. My own view, as I indicated in the introductory chapter, is that the story of the Sack of Troy was first told, toward the end of the Bronze Age, in Thessaly and other areas of northern, Aeolic Greece; and that later, perhaps during the Submycenaean period, the stories were borrowed by the descendants of the southern, Mycenaean Greeks, with whom the Aeolic Greeks were then in close and continuing contact.[1] The background of the epics, then, would have

1. Grote, *History of Greece* 2: 178–80; Adolf Holm, *The History of Greece* 4 vols. (London: Macmillan, 1906; translated from the German edition of 1885), 1: 166–68; Drews, "Argos," pp. 111–20.

been derived not only from Mycenaean Greece and from Dark
Age Ionia, but also from the less advanced Aeolic north of the
late Bronze Age.

In whatever manner the kingship of Agamemnon and of Priam might be described in the *Iliad*, the description must owe
very little to Geometric Ionia since, as we have seen, there is
no evidence that there were kings in Geometric Ionia. What
Homer had to say about kingship is likely to have taken shape
before the Ionian migration, on the Greek mainland. The pen-
etrating article on Homeric kingship by Juri Andreev concludes that for Homer, who did not know a scepter from a
gavel, traditions about kingship "abstrakte Begriffe ohne real-
en historischen Inhalt waren, die in seinen eigenen politischen
und Alltagserfahrungen keine Analogien fanden."[2] It is at least
probable that in both the Mycenaean south and in the Aeolic
north, late in the Bronze Age, there were monarchs of one kind
or another. A composite picture of the "heroic" king—some of
whose traits were taken from the Aeolic warlord, and some
from the head of the Mycenaean state—could have emerged in
Boeotia or Attica a few generations after the destruction, ca.
1200 B.C., of the great Mycenaean palaces.

Although it is methodologically perverse to use Homeric
kingship as a model for reconstructing the political institutions of Ionia during the Geometric period, there are two mat-
ters on which the epics are reliable guides. They tell us what
stories were told, and what words were used to tell them, in
eighth-century Ionia (my assumptions are that the *Iliad* was
composed ca. 750 B.C. by an Ionian for whom the name "Homer" is conventional, and that the *Odyssey* was composed ca.
700 B.C. by another poet who was probably an Ionian, but was
also familiar with the Greek mainland). By examining how a
word is used in the *Iliad* we can at least discover what that
word once meant: not necessarily in Homer's own time, but at
some point between the end of the Bronze Age and 750 B.C. In
the Hesiodic poems and in lyric, on the other hand, the mean-

2. Andreev, "Könige," p. 368.

ing of a given word can be assumed to reflect quite directly what that word meant in the author's own day. Let us see, then, what the word *basileus* meant in the Homeric epics. The question has been answered several times in several ways, most recently and thoroughly by Fritz Gschnitzer,[3] but historians have not always paid sufficient attention to the philological analyses. In a recent study, entitled *Herrschaftsformen bei Homer*, an able historian (who, however, does not appear to have known Gschnitzer's article) repeats a familiar, but incorrect, definition of Homer's *basileus:* "Er ist in der Ilias König über ein bestimmtes Territorium. . . . In der Odysee bedeutet *basileus* zunächst so wie in der Ilias 'König, Herrscher über ein bestimmtes Territorium.'"[4] Such a definition inevitably produces a plethora of kings. So, for example, Calchas' plaint at *Iliad* 1.80, κρείσσων γὰρ βασιλεύς, ὅτε χώσεται ἀνδρὶ χέρηι turns out as "Mächtiger ist nämlich der König, wenn er einem geringeren Mann zürnt."[5] Thus *basileus* is transformed not only into "a king" but into "the king."

In the *Iliad* the word *basileus* did not yet mean "king," just as the meanings of *psyche* and *Aithiopes* were not yet "soul" and "Ethiopians," no matter how regularly the words must be so translated in later Greek texts. Even in late antiquity the word *basileus* did not invariably mean "king." The English word is conventionally defined as a "hereditary male monarch," but in Hellenistic and Roman times the word was applied to certain annual magistrates as well as to the Roman emperors. The further back one goes, the greater is the divergence between the semantic fields of "king" and *basileus*. In Homeric times *basileus* had a far wider meaning than does our word "king." Through the centuries, as we shall see, it became a narrower and more exclusive term than it had been once.

3. Gschnitzer, "ΒΑΣΙΛΕΥΣ. Ein terminologischer Beitrag zur Frühgeschichte des Königtums bei den Griechen," *Innsbrucker Beiträge zur Kulturwissenschaft* 11 (1965): 99–112.

4. Sigrid Deger, *Herrschaftsformen bei Homer, Dissertationen der Universität Wien* 43 (Vienna: Verlag Notring, 1970), pp. 56, 58.

5. Deger, *Herrschaftsformen*, p. 58.

It was once thought that from an original meaning of "king" the word *basileus* was stretched, so that by Homer's time it meant sometimes "king," but sometimes only "nobleman," and that in the centuries following Homer the word tightened up again and reverted to its prestigious original meaning. This curious thesis, which has been denounced for as long a time as it has been around,[6] depends on the notion that there is a true meaning for a word, which from time to time will reassert itself against false meanings. Since there is no evidence that before Homer's time *basileus* stood for "king," the thesis must be abandoned.

Homer's *basileis* are all leaders of men, and are all "fosterlings of Zeus" (*diotrephēes*). A few of them are kings. Priam is the king of Troy, and at least in some passages Nestor appears as the king of Pylos, and Agamemnon as the king of Mycenae.[7] But many of Homer's *basileis* are not kings, which is to say that they are not hereditary monarchs. Achilles, for example, or Ajax, or Alexander are not kings, if only because Peleus, Telamon, and Priam are still alive (that Homer thought of Peleus and Telamon as kings of Phthia and Salamis is doubtful, but may be granted for the sake of the argument).[8] The Argive heroes at Troy are, without exception, all *basileis*, regardless of their position back home, and the poet often refers to them collectively as "the *basileis* of the Argives" (or of the

6. The thesis requires that originally *basileus* stood for a monarch; but as monarchy weakened during the Dark Age, more and more nobles began to call themselves *basileis*; neither the kings nor the poets, however, were concerned about the ambiguity. For objections to this thesis see Gschnitzer, "Basileus," p. 102 and n. 15.

7. For Nestor as ruler of Pylos, see *Il.* 2.77; for Priam as *anax* of Troy, see 2.373; for Agamemnon as ruler of Mycenae, see 7.180 and 11.46.

8. Although *archos* of the Myrmidon ships which he had led to Troy nine years earlier, in the *Iliad* Achilles is not king of Myrmidonland, especially since Peleus is still alive. Even Peleus, however, is at 7.126 described only as *boulēphoros* and *agorētēs* of the Myrmidons. Yet Achilles is surely a *basileus*; see, for example, 1.176, where Agamemnon tells Achilles that "of all the *basileis*, fosterlings of Zeus, thou art most hateful to me." For Alexander as *basileus* see 4.96.

Achaeans).[9] Similarly, at *Iliad* 20.84 we hear how Aeneas had boasted to the *basileis* (plural) of the Trojans. The Trojans were not ruled by a company of kings. When Homer wished to refer to Priam as the monarch of the Trojans, he used the word *anax*, which did denote a monarch.[10] Nowhere do we meet the *anaktes* (plural) of the Trojans, or the *anaktes* of the Argives. While the wider word "leader" might translate the Homeric *basileus*, the narrower words "king" and "monarch" do not. By definition, in any state there can be only one monarch. The Homeric *basileus* was not by definition exclusive: a group or a state might be led by several *basileis*.

Gschnitzer suggested that the most appropriate translation for Homer's *basileus* is "der Erste."[11] In any given community there may be several leaders, collectively called "die Ersten." But when these leaders meet together, they in turn follow a leader, who is thus "der Erste." Gschnitzer's translation is a vast improvement over "king," though it has two weaknesses: as a nominal adjective, it cannot stand without a definite article (and so the singular is inevitably exclusive), and it lacks the overtones of high birth that resound in the Homeric word *basileus*. The Latin *dux* has some of the elevation and roughly the same latitude as the Homeric *basileus*, and like the latter it appears often in military contexts. In English perhaps the best that we can come up with is a clumsy and prosaic combination, such as "highborn leader." That term is not inherently exclusive, and so we commit no oxymoron when we speak of several "highborn leaders" of a single people. On the other hand, with the addition of a definite article to the singular, "the highborn leader" is potentially exclusive.

Gschnitzer's argument against equating Homer's *basileus* with king is a sound one as far as it goes, but it does not go far enough. While insisting that *basileus* in the epics must often

---

9. For *basileis* of the Argives see 10.195; *basileis* of the Achaeans 7.106, 23.36, and 24.404. For other instances of *basileis* as a collective plural see Gschnitzer, "Basileus," p. 101, n. 8.

10. *Il.* 2.373.

11. "Basileus," p. 105.

be translated as something other than "König," Gschnitzer supposed that frequently ("nicht selten") the word does mean "König."[12] He therefore concluded that in Homer's time the word was undergoing a radical change and was well on its way to being a synonym for *anax*. If we separate the *Iliad* from the *Odyssey*, however (Gschnitzer considered them together) we shall find that in the older epic *basileus* very seldom means the (exclusive) highborn leader, and need never at all be translated as king.

All of us will agree that in order to be king you must be king of something—a state, a people, or a "bestimmtes Territorium." The same holds for the (exclusive) highborn leader. In the *Iliad*, with one exception, nobody is the *basileus* (singular) of anything. In the sole formula in which *basileus* is followed by a genitive, Agamemnon is "*basileus* of Mycenae rich in gold." This formula occurs twice, at *Iliad* 7.180 and 11.46. The latter occurrence is part of the passage which G. S. Kirk calls "the relatively late Arming of Agamemnon." The shield of Agamemnon, as described in that scene, is decorated with a Gorgon's head, a device that historians of Greek art find to have been a seventh-century innovation.[13] Other than in this formula, which could be post-Homeric, nowhere in the *Iliad* does *basileus* stand for the exclusive leader of a city or people. Of the twenty Homeric passages cited by Gschnitzer, six are from the *Odyssey*. Three more are simply invalid—at *Iliad* 6.163 Proetus is not called "König von Korinth," nor is Rhesus the "König der Thraker" at 10.435 or 10.494. In eight other passages in which *basileus* appears,[14] there is nothing to prevent giving the word an exclusive sense, but nothing to require it. Finally, at 1.277 Nestor urges Achilles not to argue with *basileus* Agamemnon, for a scepter-bearing *basileus* has far greater honor since he rules over more men. Here, surely, the scepter-bearing *basileus* must designate the exclusive leader.

12. "Basileus," p. 101.
13. *The Songs of Homer* (Cambridge: Cambridge Univ. Press, 1962), p. 186.
14. The passages cited by Gschnitzer, "Basileus," p. 101, are: 1.9, 1.231, 1.410, 4.402, 6.193, 11.23, 16.660, 19.256.

Yet even here one cannot translate the word as "king." Of course Agamemnon was a king, but so was Nestor, and both they and Achilles were all *basileis.* What set Agamemnon apart was the fact that he was commander-in-chief of all the heroes besieging Troy: Achilles and Nestor must obey Agamemnon not because he is a king, but because he is the commander.

It is also significant that in the *Iliad* we do not find the word *basileus* applied to a deity. By the sixth century, as will shortly be seen, Zeus was often called *basileus.* But for Homer he is always *anax* (as are Apollo, Hermes, and other gods). The probable reason is that in Homer's time the term *basileus* did not yet have sufficient majesty to serve as a predicate for a god, least of all for the ruler of the gods.

Yet *basileus* was potentially as lofty a title as *anax.* Although the Achaeans, or any contingent thereof, might have several *basileis,* the very logic of the word (as of any word meaning leader) pointed toward singularity and exclusiveness. The verb *basileuemen* usually occurs in singular contexts.[15] There can be many leaders present, but only one of them can actually exercise leadership at any one time. At 2.203–06 Odysseus scolds the unruly assembly:

There is no way that we all *basileusomen,* we Achaeans here. A thing with many heads is no good thing. Let there be one head, one *basileus,* to whom the son of devious Cronus has granted it.[16]

"We cannot all lead," Odysseus seems to be saying. "Let there be not many leaders, but one leader." Even the *duces* require a *dux.*

The *Odyssey* shows a slight evolution in the meaning of *basileus.* The word still most often denotes a highborn leader and not *the* highborn leader. We recall that on Ithaca there were many *basileis,* and that among the Phaeacians there were

15. Cf. 2.572 and 9.616.
16. 2.206, "Even the scepter and judgments, that he may *basileuē* among you," is bracketed by some editors.

thirteen.[17] And in the *Odyssey*, as in the *Iliad*, a god is never called *basileus*. But the word is occasionally, if still seldom, used in an exclusive sense. The clearest index of this is its association with a *nomen gentis* in the genitive case. At 4.618 and again at 15.118 we meet Phaedimus, "*basileus* of the Sidonians." At 10.110 Odysseus' companions, landed among the Laestrygonians, inquired "Who is their *basileus*?" (they learned that it was Antiphates). Pheidon, the hero, "*basileus* of the Thesprotians," appears at 14.316 and 19.287. Another indication of the nascent exclusiveness of the word is furnished by the suitors' quarrel with Telemachus. All of the suitors are *basileis*, but only one of them can hope to lead (*basileuemen*) the entire community.[18]

In the Hesiodic epics (which may be dated ca. 700 B.C.), we again rarely encounter *basileus* referring to the exclusive leader. In *Works and Days*, Hesiod inveighs against "the bribe-swallowing *basileis*" to whom a fool might bring his complaint.[19] In the *Theogony* we hear how, when a *basileus* is born, Calliope brings him eloquence so that he may become a

---

17. Compare 1.394 (Telemachus' remark that beside himself there are "many other *basileis*" in Ithaca) with 1.244–48: "For all the *aristoi* that *epikrateousin* in the isles, in Dulichium and Same and wooded Zacynthus, and as many lord it (*koiraneousi*) in rocky Ithaca, all these woo my mother and waste my house." On the Phaeacians see 8.390–91: Alcinous informs Odysseus that "there are twelve glorious *basileis* who rule among this people, and I myself am the thirteenth."

18. The passage is a notorious crux. At 1.386 Antinous rebukes Telemachus, "never may Cronion make thee *basileus* in seagirt Ithaca, which thing is of inheritance thy right." At 392–98 Telemachus responds: "Nay, verily, it is no ill thing *basileuemen*: the house of such an one quickly waxeth rich and himself is held in greater honour. Howsoever there are many other *basilēes* of the Achaeans in seagirt Ithaca, *basilēes* young and old; some one of them shall surely have this, since goodly Odysseus is dead. But as for me, I will be lord of our own house and thralls, that goodly Odysseus gat me with his spear." The explanation for the seeming confusion, as we shall see below, is that there are many *basilēes* in the nooks and crannies of a polis, but Zeus appoints only one of them "to act the *basileus*" over the whole polis.

19. *Works and Days* 37–39, 203–12, 248–73. On Hesiod's own status see Starr, *Economic and Social Growth of Early Greece*, p. 126.

good arbiter, able to settle disputes that arise in the marketplace, and a good speaker, who will be conspicuous when he speaks in the assembly (the same gifts are bestowed on a *basileus*, for the same responsibilities, by Hecate).[20] In these passages, it is generally agreed, Hesiod envisaged the *basileus* as one of several leaders, a member of a small ruling circle.[21]

Although the Hesiodic *basileus* need never be translated as "king," in two passages it does have the sense of "the (exclusive) leader." At *Theogony* 486 we find Cronus, "*basileus* of the former gods," and at *Works and Days* 668 Zeus is called "*basileus* of the immortals." In the later additions to the Hesiodic text, and therefore bracketed in most editions, there are three more references to Zeus as "*basileus* of the gods" (*Theogony* 886, 897, and 923), and one reference to Memnon as "*basileus* of the Aethiopians." A Hesiodic fragment entitles Zeus "*basileus* and *koiranos* of all."[22]

Another poem frequently dated ca. 700 B.C. or a little later is the Homeric Hymn to Demeter. Here too *basileis* are the several highborn leaders of a single community. In lines 473ff. Demeter teaches her mysteries to five *themistopolois basileusi* of Eleusis: Triptolemus, Diocles, Eumolpus, Celeus, and Polyxeinus (a sixth, mentioned at lines 153ff., was Dolichus).

---

20. *Theogony* 80–93; 434.

21. Ernst Will, "Hésiode, crise agraire? Ou recul de l'aristocratie?" *REG* 78 (1965): 542–543: "Que ces rois doivent être considérés comme les représentants de la caste des aristocrates . . . est en général admis." That Hesiod's *basilées* convened at Thespiae is undoubtedly correct, even though Hesiod never indicates the name of his polis. A few scholars have assumed that Ascra itself was Hesiod's polis, but that was a tiny place. Already deserted in Plutarch's day, the site of Ascra cannot be securely identified. Guesses center on Pyrgaki, a hill six kilometers west from Thespiae, and Listi, five kilometers north of Thespiae. See R. J. Buck, "The Site of Cerassus," *Teiresias, Proceedings of the First International Conference on Boeotian Antiquities* suppl. vol. 1 (Montreal: McGill Univ., 1972), p. 35. Since Thespiae fielded 2500 hoplites in the Persian Wars, its population must have numbered over 10,000 at that time.

22. Fr. 308, ed. Solmsen, Merkelbach, and West (Oxford: Oxford Univ. Press, 1970). See also fr. 144, where Minos, the "*basileutatos* of mortal *basileis*," rules with the scepter of Zeus.

Let us go on to the middle of the seventh century. As noted in the preceding chapter, Tyrtaeus twice makes mention of the Spartan *basileis*. At 3.3 (Diehl) he summarizes the Delphic command that "the god-honored *basileis* are to lead the council." At 4.1 he recalls "our *basileus*, Theopompus, dear to the gods." Although Tyrtaeus' *basileis* are regularly translated into English as "kings," we have seen that such a translation is not only self-contradictory (a state cannot have two monarchs), but also contradicts our historical evidence, which shows that the Spartan *basileis* were *hypeuthynoi* and that Sparta had a republican polity. There is no justification for translating Tyrtaeus' *basileus* as "king," or even as "the (exclusive) leader." In a third passage (9.7), Tyrtaeus claims that a valiant soldier is preferable to a man richer than Midas and Cinyras, or *basileuteros* than Tantalid Pelops. For Tyrtaeus, as for Homer, the splendor of lineage may have made one man *basileuteros* than another.

It was not until the late seventh and early sixth century that *basileus* began regularly to denote the exclusive leader. Mimnermus perhaps had an exclusive leader in mind when he wrote, "Even so did those alongside *basileus* charge when he commanded them, behind the screen of their hollow shields."[23] In sharp contrast with the *Iliad* and the *Odyssey*, the few hundred lines that are left of Alcaeus' poetry contain three references to Zeus as *basileus* or *pambasileus*.[24] Sappho, in speaking of the πολίων βασίληες, may have had in mind one *basileus* for each polis.[25] Four times Theognis refers to Zeus as "*basileus* of the immortals," and in a fifth passage he addresses Zeus with the vocative *basileu*.[26] There is little doubt that by the end of the sixth century the Greeks frequently used the word *basileus* to refer to the exclusive leader of a state or group. One must not

23. Mimnermus 13a in the edition of M. L. West, *Iambi et Elegi Graeci* 2 vols. (Oxford: Clarendon, 1972), vol. 2.
24. Alcaeus nos. 2 and 15 in Diehl's edition, and no. 296 in E. Lobel and D. Page, *Poetarum Lesbiorum Fragmenta* (Oxford: Clarendon, 1955).
25. Sappho no. 161 (Lobel and Page).
26. Theognis 285–86, 376, 1120, 1346.

forget, however, that even during the Classical and Hellenistic periods *basileus* was still the formal title of a variety of leaders, of whom some were lifetime generals and some were minor annual magistrates.

In common parlance, *basileus* eventually was used only with an exclusive sense. Even in Roman times, however, *basileus* was not quite the equivalent of "king" or "monarch." Hadrian was a *basileus*, but we would not call him a king or a monarch. Today, the modern Greek *basileus* or *vasilyás* is equivalent to the English "king," but the congruence was long in coming.

This review tells us something about the political history of Archaic Greece. When in the eighth and seventh centuries the Greeks of this or that state conferred upon a magistrate the title of *basileus*, they could not have done so out of nostalgia for an old kingly title. For the word did not come to mean "king" until long after these magistracies were established. The often repeated generalization that the republican *basileiai* had survived from monarchical regimes of the Geometric period not only is without historical basis, but also has no philological basis.[27]

We can also now appreciate what an innovation the Archaic *basileia* (or the *prytaneia*) must have been. The republican *basileus* was not an emasculated replica of an earlier monarch.

---

27. This assumption, despite what has been learned about the word *basileus*, still flourishes. See, for example, R. Sealey, *A History of the Greek City States*, p. 24: "In sedentary conditions the relations between king, council and assembly changed. . . . Although in some cities an office with the title of king (*basileus*) was kept, its authority decreased; sometimes the office became elective and its term was limited to one year. . . . Thus at Athens by ca. 632 and perhaps much earlier the monarchy had been replaced by an annual board of nine elective officials; one of them bore the title of king." Pavel Oliva, "*Patrike basileia*," p. 179, found in the Athenian magistrate's title evidence that the old kingship had been peacefully replaced by aristocracy: "That the function of *basileus*, however, was not even in Athens abolished by violence is proved, beside tradition about the creation of the archontate, by the fact that even later the *basileus* remained one of the highest Athenian officials."

Quite the contrary, the Archaic *basileus* (or, in Miletus, Corinth, and elsewhere, the *prytanis*[28]) must have been the very first head of state in the history of the polis, and the creation of such an office represented an unprecedented concentration of authority in the hands of one individual. That the polis had any head of state was still a novelty in the late eighth century. For the word *basileus*, like the words *archon* and *prytanis*, was originally a nonexclusive word for leader, and in 700 B.C. was just beginning to designate *the* leader of a community.

Our review also suggests, as the opposite side of the coin, something about the government of a Greek polis in the Geometric period. Hesiod, in both the *Works and Days* and the *Theogony*, implies a government in the hands of several *basileis*. Since both the *Odyssey* and the Homeric Hymn to Demeter attribute the same state of affairs to the heroic past, it is a safe assumption that during the Geometric period each polis had looked to several *basileis* for leadership. There will have been no higher position, no title that transcended that of the *basileis*, and so no head of state in a polis of Geometric Greece. That is not to say that the several *basileis* in a given polis must always have acted as a group. In battle all might have had positions of leadership, but surely one *basileus* would have been designated as commander-in-chief. It is probable, however, that this singular leadership ended with the battle, and that in peacetime the several highborn leaders stood on the same level.

How this informal leadership of the *basileis* may have originated is not difficult to imagine. Both Gschnitzer and Andreev assume, and the assumption is undoubtedly correct, that during the Late Helladic III B period the *basileis* were subordinate officials in each of the several large states into which Mycenaean Greece seems to have been divided.[29] Gschnitzer sup-

---

28. On the Milesian *prytanis* see Aristotle *Pol.* 1305a. Cf. Gschnitzer, s.v. Prytanis, *RE Supplement* XIII, 733–34.

29. Gschnitzer, "Basileus," pp. 110–11; Andreev, "Könige," p. 379; cf. also Thomas, "From Wanax to Basileus," pp. 190–91.

posed that each large Mycenaean state broke apart into a handful of *poleis*, and that each of these *poleis* was during the Dark Age led by a single *basileus*.[30] Andreev, on the other hand, proposed that after the destruction of ca. 1200 B.C. and the subsequent migrations, Greece was fragmented into a multitude of tiny principalities—each valley or village being an independent *Fürstentum*—and that each of these tiny units was headed by a *basileus*. In the eighth century, Andreev continues, in one area after another, neighboring principalities tended to coalesce and to form a polis; and thus, by a process of *synoikismos*, there arose the *poleis* of historical times. These *poleis*, to conclude this summary of Andreev's thesis, were governed by aristocratic regimes: the *basileus* of each principality exchanged, in the eighth century, his minuscule monarchy for a share in the control of a much larger state.[31]

Andreev's reconstruction, however, is entirely theoretical, resting on neither literary nor archaeological evidence. In the eastern Aegean the Ionian and Aeolian settlements seem not to have gone through a development from multiple *Fürstentümer* to single polis. Archaeological evidence indicates that in the ninth century Smyrna, at least, was apparently a unitary com-

---

30. Gschnitzer, "Basileus," pp. 107–09.

31. Andreev, "Könige," p. 380, n. 50, believes that his thesis was anticipated by G. M. Calhoun, "Classes and Masses in Homer," *CP* 29 (1934): 301–16. In fact, Calhoun's understanding of the *basileus* was quite different from Andreev's. Calhoun concluded that nothing in the Homeric poems "is incompatible with the rather simple tribal monarchy which appears, both from the archaeological record and from the Greek tradition, to have been a common form of social organization prior to the rise of aristocracies" (p. 314). Calhoun, like Andreev, imagined that before the polis came into being the *basileus* ruled his little *Fürstentum*; but Calhoun also, quite unlike Andreev, imagined that the polis itself, once it had come into being, was ruled by a king, whose council was made up of all the petty *basileis* whose "kingdoms" had been absorbed into the polis. See especially, p. 313: "The petty kings, originally independent, become first the 'elders' of the king's council. . . . Later with the increasing importance of agriculture and the accumulation of large estates, they constitute a landed nobility which encroaches upon the powers of the king by appointing magistrates to share his functions."

munity.³² For the Peloponnese and Central Greece the Catalogue of Ships shows that *poleis* existed already in the Late Helladic III period. According to the catalogue, which was probably composed in the Submycenaean period, each Mycenaean state was made up of several *poleis*. So, for example, the Arcadian troops (who filled sixty ships and were led by Agapenor) came from nine localities, each of which was apparently called a polis (*ptolis, ptoliethron*). Agapenor's Arcadians were all those

that dwelt in Pheneos and Orchomenos abounding in flocks, and Rhipe and Stratie and windy Enispe, and that possessed Tegea and lovely Mantineia, and possessed Stymphelos and dwelt in Parrhasie.³³

The epithets suggest that in Mycenaean times a *ptolis* was not a town (to say nothing of a city), but a rural citadel and the countryside that surrounded it.³⁴ At any rate, many of the *poleis* of historical Greece—Thespiae and Plataea, Chalcis and Eretria, Corinth and Sicyon, and a hundred others—were in existence long before the Catalogue of Ships was composed. That the typical polis of mainland Greece arose in the eighth century, through a unification of small principalities, is therefore out of the question. As for a *synoikismos* in eighth-century Attica, whether a political re-unification or the creation of an urban center, Attica was not a typical state.³⁵

Gschnitzer's belief that the historical *poleis* emerged at the beginning, rather than at the end, of the Dark Age fits much better with the literary and archaeological evidence. But there is no support for Gschnitzer's belief that through the Dark Age the

32. See especially J. M. Cook, "Greek Settlement in the Eastern Aegean and Asia Minor," pp. 796–804.

33. *Iliad* 2.605–08.

34. D. R. Cole, "*Asty* and *Polis:* "City" in Early Greek" (Ph.D. diss., Stanford Univ., 1976), concluded that "in the late Bronze Age *polis* meant 'citadel *asty*, 'lower residential town.'"

35. On *synoikismos* see P. Musiolek, "Zum Begriff und zur Bedeutung des Synoikismos," *Klio* 63 (1981): 207–13; see also R. A. Padgug, "Eleusis and the Union of Attica," *GRBS* 13 (1972): 135–50.

nascent polis was ruled by a monarchical *basileus*.[36] As we have seen in tedious detail, the evidence for such monarchs is either contrived or missing altogether. In addition, Gschnitzer's thesis does nothing to explain why the early poets portray states of both the present (Thespiae) and the remote past (Scheria, Ithaca, Eleusis) as having many *basileis*. Finally, we have seen that in the early epics the use of *basileus* in an exclusive sense is extraordinary.[37] If *basileis* were the leaders of Geometric *poleis*, and everything indicates that they were, then the Geometric polis regularly had no single head of state.

Let us speculate, then, about the origins of the Dark Age regime of the *basileis*. Let us say, with Andreev, that in the Mycenaean period the *basileus* held a very circumscribed position. In any Mycenaean state there would have been a great many *basileis:* not four or five, but forty or fifty. Let us say also, this time with Gschnitzer, that when the Mycenaean palace and state were shattered, what survived the ruin were the various *poleis* that had made up the Late Helladic III state.

36. I have cited Gschnitzer here because his article develops the thesis most purposefully and clearly. That in the Dark Age a *basileus* was monarch of the polis—however rudimentary the polis may then have been—is of course commonly assumed, not only in general treatments of the period but also in specialized articles. Starr, "Decline of the Early Greek Kings," pp. 132–34, although occasionally speaking of "tribal chieftains," tends to locate the *basileis* in *poleis* (Syracuse, Sparta, and Argos are mentioned). Thomas, "Roots of Homeric Kingship," pp. 400–07, also pictures a Dark Age *basileus* ruling over a polis, especially in Asia Minor; among her examples are Chios, Ephesus, and Cyme. I am not able to decide whether Oliva, "Patrike basileia," pp. 176ff., visualizes the *basileus* as ruler of a polis or as tribal chief. On p. 176 he states that "the tribal system in its ultimate phase, therefore, is the basis of the social position held by the early Greek *basileis*." When this abstract generalization becomes specific, on p. 179, the tribes seem to turn into *poleis:* "So the *basileis* of Ephesus, Corinth, Athens, and other communities, were just as Homer's *basileis* chieftains of tribes or tribal confederacies, supreme representatives of the tribal system which was then the social organization in Greece."

37. According to Gschnitzer's thesis, the term *basileus* already in Homer's time frequently stood for king, and therefore by Homer's time must have for many generations been in use as a title for kings. Gschnitzer's second conclusion was based squarely on the first.

But leadership in each polis fell not to a single *basileus* but to the several *basileis* for whom that polis provided protection. The several *basileis*, during the Dark Age, would have supplied whatever leadership the orphaned polis needed, especially by rallying to the defense of the citadel or by fighting in the vanguard when their *politai* attacked a neighboring polis. The evolution sketched above does not depend on, but is tailored to, what is known of the *pa-si-re-u* (or *qa-si-re-u*) of the Linear B tablets. Linguists believe, even though they cannot prove, that the *pa-si-re-u* of the tablets is the same word as the *basileus* of alphabetic Greek.[38] At Pylos and at Cnossus individuals holding the title *pa-si-re-u* are attested. From the tablets at Cnossus three (another interpretation yields nine) persons are so identified.[39] At Pylos the number is at least nine, and possibly twelve.[40] And of course there is no reason to think that the tablets which have been found contain the names of all, or even most, of a kingdom's officials. Unfortunately, no tablet indicates the size of the area managed by a *pa-si-re-u*. Hierarchically, the *pa-si-re-u* seems to have stood on a level with the *po-ro-ko-re-te*, presumably the deputy for the *ko-re-te* (usually regarded either as a "district chief" or a village "mayor").[41] These minor officials were provincial, that is,

38. John Chadwick, *The Decipherment of Linear B*, 2nd ed. (Cambridge: Cambridge Univ. Press, 1967), p. 115; Denys Page, *History and the Homeric Iliad* (Berkeley: Univ. of California Press, 1959), pp. 186; 208, n. 40. For objections to the identification see L. R. Palmer, "Linear B Texts of Economic Interest," *Serta Philologica Aenipontana, Innsbrucker Beiträge zur Kulturwissenschaft* 7–8 (1962), pp. 1–12. Gschnitzer, "Basileus," pp. 99–100, points out that Palmer's objections are based on semantic rather than linguistic considerations, especially the assumption that *basileus* means king and the fact that *pa-si-re-u* does not.

39. Gschnitzer, "Basileus," p. 110, n. 35.

40. M. Lejeune, "Les forgerons de Pylos," *Historia* 10 (1961): 422, counts nine. For the larger figure see T. B. L. Webster, *From Mycenae to Homer*, 2nd ed. (New York: Norton, 1964), p. 15.

41. Gschnitzer, "Basileus," p. 111. Of the *ko-re-te* officials, Webster suggests that "we may regard them as the mayors of . . . villages or towns" (*From Mycenae to Homer*, p. 15).

they were in residence not in the palace itself but in various parts of the kingdom.[42] It is therefore not too bold a hypothesis that when Pylos (and other great palaces) were destroyed, the *pa-si-re-u* officials survived, and that small groups of them collaborated to give leadership to a community centered on a polis. In Attica, where the Mycenaean state was able to hold together during the Dark Age, even though the *wanax* and his palace had disappeared, there may have been a great many *basileis*. In a typical polis, the number will have been much smaller. The poets imagined five *basileis* in the Eleusis of Triptolemus' day and thirteen at Scheria.

We may also conclude that through the Geometric period the *basileis* constituted a well defined caste. Here the Linear B tablets are of no help, for we do not know how a *pa-si-re-u* came by his position. At the other end of the Dark Age, however, there is no doubt that the *basileis* inherited their status. Lineage, and a special relation to the gods, are characteristic of all *basileis*. Homer's favorite epithet for them, *diotrephēes*, implies that from their birth the *basileis* are the recipients of Zeus' favor and protection; this is the more natural since ultimately Homer's *basileis* are descended from the race of the gods. Tyrtaeus describes Sparta's *basileis* as "dear to the gods" or "god-honored." Even Hesiod, who complained about them, conceded to the *basileis* their entitlement. When they are not "gift-devouring," Hesiod's *basileis* are either *diotrephēes* (*Theog.* 82) or *aidoioi* (*Theog.* 80; 434). The latter epithet puts them in good company, for the very race of the gods is *aidoion* (*Theog.* 44). The hereditary nature of the *basileis*' position is also indicated by the title held by their mothers, wives, and daughters. A *basileia* must have the same lofty lineage as her husband if the couple is to produce offspring dear to the gods. It is worth noting that the

---

42. Cf. Page, *History and the Homeric Iliad*, p. 186: "There is one tablet which suggests that in Crete the *basileus* occupied a post in provincial towns comparable with that of the *lawagetas* in the capital." In the Pylos tablets, Lejeune ("Les forgerons," p. 422) observes, a *pa-si-re-u*, to whom smiths make their deliveries of metal, is regularly identified with a toponym, presumably the name of a village. "Autant qu'on puisse le voir, dans l'état pylien, les βασιλεῖς etaient des dignitaires provinciaux d'importance secondaires."

title *basileia* is found not only in Homer's heroic society, but also in historical Athens. The wife of the annual *basileus* was always the *basilissa*,[43] even though there was no special title or status for the wives of archons, polemarchs, or generals. The informal regime of the *basileis*, it would appear, persisted well into the eighth century. Perhaps ca. 750 B.C., and perhaps under the stimulus of eastern models (one thinks of the polity which the Phoenicians established at Carthage), the Greeks began finding it expedient to institute a more formal structure. Instead of having an indefinite number of leaders all more or less on the same level, and a commander-in-chief in time of emergency, a polis would now establish definite positions of leadership: it would have one year round leader, or two leaders (as at Sparta), or three leaders (as the Athenians' archon, *basileus*, and polemarch). However many there were, the positions would be demarcated and procedures for filling them would be established. In short, the inefficiency and confusion that must have attended "a thing with many heads" were replaced by order and by institutions, by magistracies and councils, and by a *politeia*.

An exploration of the eighth-century innovations, however, is beyond the scope of this monograph, the focus of which has been the regimes that preceded the Archaic aristocracies. On these we have reached a tentative conclusion. In the conventional picture of the Geometric period, the Greek state is centered on a king, upon whose powers the nobles are gradually encroaching. The evidence, historical and lexical, suggests a rather different picture: the Greek polis in the Geometric period has no king and is led by a small circle of hereditary leaders, the *basileis*. It remains to be seen how and why, by the end of the Archaic period, the word *basileus* may have come to stand primarily for a state's exclusive hereditary leader.

43. The word *basileia* is invariably translated into English as "queen"; while that translation is appropriate for the fifth century, it is somewhat premature for the eighth. In the *Iliad* Hecuba, who is certifiably a queen, is never called *basileia*. The term is used in the *Odyssey* for Tyro, Nausicaa, Arete (three times), and Penelope (twelve times).

CHAPTER IV   THE HEREDITARY *BASILEIS* OF THE ARCHAIC AND CLASSICAL PERIODS

There is no credible evidence of kings in the Greek *poleis* of the Geometric period. And we have seen that *basileus* came to stand for the exclusive leader of a state during the Archaic period. The question arises, What gave to this old word its new meaning? A fairly obvious answer is that the new meaning came about when the old word was applied to new institutions.

In a backwater such as Hesiod's Thespiae the *basileis* may still have been, long after 700 B.C., the group of princes who without much formal machinery governed the little Boeotian *polis*. These leaders might very well be called collectively "the *basileis* of the Thespians," but no one of them could be called "the *basileus* of the Thespians." But at some point the word *basileus* began to be used as a technical term for an official—in some cases the chief official—of a polis. Not all *poleis*, of course, used the same term for their chief magistrates. In some states we find a *prytanis* at the head, in others an archon. These terms also had the generic meaning of chief or leader. The significant point for our purposes, however, is that these terms were used as titles for particular offices. By "title" I do not mean an appellation constitutionally designated, but one rigidly maintained by tradition (and for all practical purposes therefore inseparable from the institution). Thus although all three terms might in the Archaic period continue to have a generic meaning which we might translate as prince or leader, they also now have a technical meaning, for which transliteration rather than translation is appropriate. So, for example, at *Politics* 1322b, discussing the officials who offer sacrifices, Aristotle observes that custom prescribed priests as the sacrificers for various cults, but for others designated "those men who derive their dignity from the common hearth: some call these men archons, some call them *basileis*, and others call them *prytaneis*."

The term *basileus* was used for various officials. We have noted a college of *basileis* at Chios, at Mytilene, and apparently at Aeolian Cyme. In addition to these *poleis* already mentioned, there is evidence for a college of *basileis* at Athens, at Cyzicus, at Siphnos, and possibly at Cos.[1] The character and function of most of these colleges can only be guessed at, since even for Athens it is not certain who were the *basileis* of the college, or what their duties were.[2]

Single officials were also given the title of *basileus*. An annual official such as the *basileus* at Athens is attested for a number of states: Abdera, Chios, Ephesus, Ios, Megara, Miletus, Naxos, and Samothrace.[3] These officials, presumably,

1. For documentation see Busolt, *Staatskunde* 1:351, nn. 2–6; and Gschnitzer, "Basileus," p. 103, n. 19.

2. Ronald S. Stroud, *Drakon's Law on Homicide* (Berkeley: Univ. of California Press, 1968), pp. 45–47, discusses the problem of the *basileis* at Athens, the earliest mention of whom comes in l. 12 of the 409/8 B.C. copy of Draco's law. Stroud concludes, p. 47, that in that law the *basileis* are not the *phylobasileis* but rather the annual *basileus* and "the successive holders of this annual office."

3. The *basileus* at Athens is conveniently referred to by scholars as "the archon-basileus," since he belonged to the board of nine headed by the archon; but in Greek sources he is always the *basileus*, never the *archon-basileus*. Documentation on *basileis* outside of Athens is given by Gschnitzer, "Basileus," p. 110, n. 32. Gschnitzer's attribution of an annual *basileus* to Mantinea rests entirely on *P.Oxy.* XI, no. 1367, which describes Demonax

were severally referred to as "the *basileus* of the Abderites," "the *basileus* of the Chians," and so forth. What they did is not clear. It is not impossible that the Megarian *basileus* commanded the army in the Archaic period, though not if, as S. I. Oost has argued, there was a polemarch at Megara. Aristotle's remark shows that religious duties were frequently given to the annual *basileus*. In Athens a judicial function was added to the religious one, and some scholars have suggested that in the Archaic period the *basileus* regularly presided over the Council of the Areopagus.[4]

In the last chapter it was suggested that through most of the Geometric period the typical polis was governed by a group of *basileis*, and that only toward the end of the period was a single magistrate appointed over the entire state. The man who held this position—whether called *basileus*, archon, or *prytanis*—must have enjoyed unprecedented power and prestige. In the late Archaic period (after the heyday of the tyrants) the *poleis* went to some lengths to divide responsibilities among several officials, lest one individual attain too much personal power. The result was often a board of co-equal magistrates, as the eight *probouloi* in post-Cypselid Corinth and the six (or nine) *damiorgoi* in post-Pheidonian Argos. In Athens the nine so-called archons (in fact, one archon, a *basileus*, a polemarch, and six *thesmothetai*) undoubtedly antedated Pisistratus'

(whom we shall discuss presently) as "*basileus* of the Mantineans." The papyrus comes from Heraclides Lembus' epitome of Hermippus' *On Lawgivers*, and should not be preferred to Herodotus who describes Demonax simply as "a most highly regarded citizen" of Mantinea (4.161). A. A. I. Waisglass, "Demonax, βασιλεὺς Μαντινέων," *AJP* 77 (1956): 167–76, argued that Demonax was an annual *basileus*, but surely Heraclides intended to say that Demonax was a king. We have noted that Amphidamas of Chalcis, who is not a king in Hesiod's *Works and Days*, was promoted to "King of Euboea" by the author of the *Certamen*.

4. Robert Bonner and Gertrude Smith, *The Administration of Justice from Homer to Aristotle*, 2 vols. (Chicago: Univ. of Chicago Press, 1930), 1: 94. The argument depends in part, however, on the assumption that the annual *basileus* inherited the powers which in the Geometric period belonged to a king.

coup, though not necessarily the threat of tyranny, made vivid in Cylon's abortive coup of ca. 628 B.C.

But in the early Archaic period it was apparently the rule for a polis to have one magistrate who was recognizably the head of state. Aristotle concluded that this practice was one of the causes of tyranny. At *Pol.* 1305a he states that

> there were more tyrannies in earlier times than now because certain people were entrusted with great offices; as happened in Miletus, for example, from the office of the *prytanis* (for the *prytanis* was in charge of many and important matters.)

The reference, presumably, was to Thrasybulus. Generalizing again on the matter at *Pol.* 1310b, Aristotle says that some tyrannies

> arose from those people elected to the highest offices (for in ancient times the people set a long tenure for the public and sacred offices), and other tyrannies arose out of oligarchies, which selected one man to be in charge of the chief offices.

As examples of the latter Aristotle mentions "the Ionian tyrants and Phalaris."

The phenomenon of one magistrate over the entire polis seems to have been remarkable enough for the Greeks of the early Archaic period that they coined a word for the single leader: *monarchos.* This was usually not a title, though it is attested as a title in fourth-century Cos. And, as a recent study has argued, the title of *monarchos* must have been fixed at Cos early in the Archaic period, before the word became the pejorative that it was in Solon's time.[5] There is even seventh-century evidence for the negative connotations of the word. Herodotus (5.92) recites an oracle supposedly delivered before Cypselus was born, but almost necessarily fashioned after (though per-

---

5. Susan M. Sherwin-White, *Ancient Cos* (Göttingen: Vandenhoeck & Ruprecht, 1978; = *Hypomnemata, 51*), pp. 192–93. See also Elizabeth Farmer Craik, "Two Notes on Officials at Kos," *Parola del Passato* 22 (1967): 443–45, and G. Pugliese Carratelli, "Ancora sul monarchos di Cos," pp. 446–50 in the same volume.

haps soon after) Cypselus had overthrown the Bacchiad oligarchy. Apollo promised that Aetion and Labda would have a son who would fall like a rock on the ἀνδράσι μουνάρχοισι, a phrase that seems to mean "the men who govern as single leaders" and so refers to the office of *prytanis*.[6] The tone of the oracle suggests that not all Corinthians looked kindly upon the Bacchiads' practice of elevating one of their number to an annual chief magistracy. Quite clearly, the single chief magistrates of the early Archaic period were not self-effacing holders of the office. Some of them seem to have used the position as a steppingstone to tyranny, and perhaps others used it to lord it over the citizenry, at the least taking on airs and enjoying their unwonted eminence. Thus one can imagine the word *basileus* also taking on connotations of exclusiveness in the Archaic period. The man who held the title "*basileus* of the Athenians" was surely, at least for the year, a respected figure throughout Athens. In those states in which the annual *basileus* held wider powers his τιμή would have been correspondingly greater.

There was another magistrate, far more conspicuous than the annual officials, who in the Archaic and Classical periods went under the title of *basileus*. The hereditary and lifelong *basileis* were undoubtedly rare figures, but their presence (though limited) was significant: in the Geometric period it seems that no individual had risen to such personal prominence in the *poleis*.

As noted in the second chapter, there is considerable evidence for a hereditary *basileia* at Argos. It seems to have existed already in the late eighth century, and it was still there in the middle of the fifth century. The main responsibilities of the Argive *basileus* were apparently military and diplomatic. The Agiads and Eurypontids of Sparta must also, of course, be included among the hereditary *basileis:* they were in essence,

6. The usual translation, "men who rule alone" (cf. Forrest, *Emergence of Greek Democracy*, p. 111; Bury and Meiggs, *History of Greece*, p. 106) does not bring out the numerical meaning of *mounos:* one, single.

as Aristotle phrased it (*Pol.* 1285a), "plenipotentiary and permanent generals," although they too played an important role in diplomacy and in internal affairs. Although we do not know that the Tarentines had a hereditary *basileia*, the probability is that they did, and that it was patterned after the *basileia* in Sparta (except that the Tarentines may have had a single *basileus*). A number of Cretan *poleis*, according to Aristotle (*Pol.* 1272a), once had *basileis*, but the Cretans abolished the office and gave the military command to the *kosmoi*. And we have seen that there may have been something of the sort at Samos.

The Spartan *basileia* was the most durable and is the most fully described in our sources, but perhaps a more impressive *basileia* in Archaic and Classical Greece was the one at Cyrene. Established at the foundation of the city, traditionally 631 B.C.,[7] the Cyrenaean *basileia* continued until at least 454 B.C. and probably, as F. Chamoux proposed, until ca. 440 B.C.[8]

The Cyrenaean *basileia* is usually looked upon as a bird out of season, a throwback to the Dark Age, when all Greek *poleis* are supposed to have been ruled by kings. This understanding of the Cyrenaean *basileia* is not surprising, since there has been such a widespread tendency to translate *basileus* as king: if one finds a *basileus*, one has found either a monarchy or its vestiges. As the title of his book indicates, Chamoux believed that Cyrene was governed by a monarchy for almost two centuries. He referred to the regime not only as "la monarchie," but even (at least until the reform of Demonax, ca. 550 B.C.) as a "royauté absolue."[9] The assumption with which Chamoux started, and did not examine, was that when the Theraeans founded Cyrene they gave to the city a primitive government, the kind which in most Greek states was supposedly superseded in the eighth or early seventh century. The Theraeans

7. Eratosthenes, who was a Cyrenaean, was responsible for the date. On its general accuracy see François Chamoux, *Cyrène sous la monarchie des Battiades* (Paris: Boccard, 1953), p. 121.

8. Chamoux, *Cyrène*, pp. 205–06.

9. Chamoux, *Cyrène*, pp. 141–42.

instituted a primitive monarchy in Cyrene, Chamoux believed, because they themselves still had such a regime in 631
B.C.

Upon examination, however, it appears that neither Thera
nor Cyrene had a monarchy, absolute or otherwise, in the second half of the seventh century. What Thera had was a *basileus*
named Grinnus, whose position was hereditary and who
claimed descent, according to Herodotus (4.147.2) from the
maternal uncle of Eurysthenes and Procles at Sparta. And the
Theraean regime was not at all a primitive survival, but was
surprisingly au courant. We learn of Grinnus through a famous
Herodotean *logos:*

> Up to this point in the story the Lacedaemonians and Theraeans say
> the same thing; but from here on only the Theraeans say things hap-
> pened this way. Grinnus the son of Aesanius, a descendant of the
> above-mentioned Theras, and being the *basileus* of the island of
> Thera, went off to Delphi with a hecatomb from the polis. Accom-
> panying him were others of the citizens and especially Battus son of
> Polymnestus, who was by ancestry a Euphemid, of the Minyae. When
> Grinnus the *basileus* of the Theraeans was consulting the oracle on
> other matters, the Pythian priestess directed him to found a polis in
> Libya. But he answered in the following words: 'O *Anax,* I am now too
> old and settled to get up and go off. Command one of these younger
> men to do this.' When he said this he pointed to Battus. [4.150]

As it happened, when the Theraeans eventually sent off to
Libya two penteconters full of colonists, they decided that
"Battus should be their *hēgēmon* and *basileus.*" Herodotus'
story does not show that Grinnus was monarch of Thera. He
was descended from the island's eponymous hero, was surely
in charge of the state's religious apparatus, and undoubtedly
had other responsibilities as well. But Herodotus does not
seem to have thought of him as king of Thera. For Herodotus
did not regard it as unthinkable that Grinnus should go off
from Thera as an oikist, an assignment that no monarch could
be expected to undertake.

But we need not depend entirely on an exegesis of the Herodotean text. Other evidence on the government of the

Theraeans at the time they founded Cyrene is supplied by the so-called Foundation Decree of Cyrene. This Cyrenaean inscription from the first half of the fourth century purports to convey the Theraeans' original decree providing for the creation of the Libyan colony.[10] That a seventh-century decree was available for copying in fourth-century Cyrene is possible, but perhaps it is more likely that the decree was constructed in the early fourth century, from an assortment of oral, epigraphic, and literary sources.[11] Chamoux, calling the inscription a forgery, decided to discount it entirely. That one cannot do. The decree at any rate reflects what the early fourth-century Cyrenaeans thought about the foundation of their city, and it is therefore a source of considerable importance. Significantly, Chamoux decided that the inscription was a worthless source precisely because it presented the decision to colonize as originating not with King Grinnus but with an assembly:

On ne voit guère comment la monarchie, qui était certainement encors le régime en vigueur dans l'île, aurait pu laisser la décision à l'assemblée du peuple dans une affaire aussi grave. Ce décret doit donc avoir été forgé postérieurement, à une époque où il était tout naturel que la fondation d'une colonie dépendît de l'*ecclesia*.[12]

In short, Chamoux presupposed that because it had a *basileus*, Thera in 631 B.C. was a monarchy, and he therefore rejected as a forgery a document which did not present it as a monarchy.

    Let us proceed instead on the assumption that what Herodotus and the early fourth-century Cyrenaeans thought about

    10. For the inscription see Meiggs and Lewis, *Greek Historical Inscriptions*, no. 5. The first twenty-two lines of the inscription present a fourth-century decree of the Cyrenaean *damos*, granting citizenship to Theraeans resident in Cyrene; appended to this decree is the so-called Foundation Decree. On the date, see Chamoux, *Cyrène*, p. 105.

    11. There is a growing tendency to see the Foundation Decree as a re-editing, in fourth-century language, of a genuine seventh-century decree. Arguments presented by A. J. Graham, "The Authenticity of the ὅρϰιον τῶν οἰϰιστήρων of Cyrene," *JHS* 80 (1960): 94–111; and L. H. Jeffery, "The Pact of the First Settlers at Cyrene," *Historia* 10 (1961):139–47.

    12. Chamoux, *Cyrène*, p. 110.

the foundation of Cyrene is as good a guide as we are likely to find on the subject. If the Cyrenaeans thought that their city was founded after a decree of the Theraean ecclesia, then the Cyrenaeans did not think that in 631 B.C. Thera was ruled by a monarchy. The relevant portion of the inscription, adapted from A. J. Graham's translation, follows:

> Decided by the assembly. Since Apollo has given a spontaneous prophecy to Battus and the Theraeans ordering them to colonize Cyrene, the Theraeans resolve that Battus be sent to Libya as *archagetas* and *basileus*.[13]

The Spartan *basileis*, it will be recalled, were also referred to as *archagetai*. That the Theraean regime was modelled on that of Sparta is very likely. The Theraeans' story was that their ancestors had come from Sparta in heroic times. But Dorians probably did not reach Thera until after 1000 B.C., and perhaps not until ca. 700 B.C. At any rate, the Theraeans were apparently keen to imitate the Spartans and their *eunomia*. We have already noted evidence for ephors at Thera.[14]

The inscription also has implications about the government of early Cyrene. Chamoux assumed, with good reason, that the city's institutions—what Thucydides (6.5.1) would call *nomima*—were derived from those at Thera. There is ample proof that, in the words of A. J. Graham, "it was normal for the colony to continue the cults, calendar, dialect, script, state offices, and citizen divisions of the mother city."[15] If, then, the fourth-century Cyrenaeans believed that an ecclesia governed ancient Thera, it was probably because they believed that Cyrene itself had from the beginning been under the control of its ecclesia.

As is the case with so many *poleis*, there is very little evi-

13. Except for the retention of the technical terms, the translation is that given by Graham, *Colony and Mother City in Ancient Greece* (New York: Barnes and Noble, Inc., 1964), p. 225.

14. F. Hiller von Gaertringen, "Alt-Thera vor der Gründung von Kyrene," *Klio* 33 (1940):68. For evidence on ephors at Thera see above p. 80, n. 87.

15. Graham, *Colony and Mother City*, p. 14.

dence on the institutions of Archaic Cyrene. There is some information on the constitution approved by Ptolemy I in 322 B.C., and it is probable that Ptolemy did not greatly disturb the existing machinery. Ptolemaic Cyrene had an ecclesia and two councils (one a gerousia and the other referred to as the *boulē*). The gerousia is also attested for Classical Cyrene and for her colony at Euhesperides,[16] and it is therefore reasonable to assume a gerousia in Archaic Cyrene. Ephors are also attested at Cyrene and Euhesperides, and Chamoux is undoubtedly correct in supposing that they too were there from the founding of Cyrene.[17] The ecclesia is not mentioned until the fourth century, and Chamoux supposed that it was not established until the "monarchie" was abolished ca. 440 B.C.[18] As suggested above, however, the early fourth-century foundation decree implies that the Cyrenaeans regarded an ecclesia as a normal institution of state. That the ecclesia in Cyrene was a recent innovation when the inscription was made is quite improbable. It is likely that from the beginning Cyrene had an ecclesia, a gerousia, ephors, and a *basileus.*

What position did the *basileus* hold in the government of Cyrene? From 631 B.C. until Demonax of Mantinea was summoned to reform the state, the *basileus* played a considerably greater role than he did in later years. For according to Herodotus (4.161) one of the two principal reforms of ca. 550 B.C. was the restriction of the *basileus:*

Arcesilas' son Battus succeeded him, being lame and unsteady on his feet. Because of the disaster that they had just suffered, the Cyrenaeans sent to Delphi to inquire in what way they might arrange things so as to fare the best. The Pythia ordered them to fetch a fixer from Mantinea in Arcadia. The Cyrenaeans accordingly made a request, and the Mantineans sent a most highly regarded citizen whose name was Demonax. When he got to Cyrene and learned the situation

16. Chamoux, *Cyrène,* pp. 214, 216.
17. Chamoux, *Cyrène,* p. 215. Evidence for ephors at Cyrene: *SEG* IX, no. 1 (line 33), and Heraclides Lembus fr. 18 (ed. Dilts); for the ephors at Euhesperides see P. M. Fraser, *Gnomon* 29 (1957):18, n. 1.
18. Chamoux, *Cyrène,* p. 216.

in detail, first of all he divided them into three tribes. . . . Secondly, he reserved for the *basileus* Battus the *temenē* and priesthoods, but everything else that earlier *basileis* had had Demonax put at the disposal of the people (ἐς μέσον τῷ δήμῳ ἔθηκε).

The most important responsibility that the *basileus* lost in Demonax' reform was very likely the command of the army. The disaster that had led to Demonax' visit occurred when Arcesilas II (ca. 568–52 B.C.) led the Cyrenaeans to a total defeat at the hands of the Libyans, 7000 Cyrenaeans supposedly losing their lives in the battle.[19] After Demonax' reform we hear no more of the *basileus* as Cyrene's commander-in-chief. Perhaps it was Demonax who instituted the board of *strategoi* which appears in later evidence.[20]

The *basileus* also, as in Sparta, had a seat in the gerousia. One of the outlandish actions of Pheretima, mother of Arcesilas III, was her usurpation of this position that had rightfully been her son's.[21] And, as shown by the passage quoted above, the *basileus* was the chief religious officer of Cyrene. Altogether it appears that initially the Cyrenaean *basileus* had a position very similar to that of the Spartan *basileis*, and it is not impossible that not long before the Theraeans installed their regime at Cyrene, the Theraeans themselves had established on their island a *politeia* on the Spartan model. The Cyrenaeans in the fifth century, as an ode of Pindar shows, took pride in being descended, via Thera, from the Spartans.[22]

But the *basileia* at Cyrene, unlike the Spartan prototype, was not a static institution. Diodorus (8.30) says that the first *basileus*, Battus, had governed democratically and had been satisfied, as Diodorus saw it, "with just the title of king." His successors, Diodorus continues, became ever more tyrannical, and the same impression is given in Herodotus' narrative. There is also graphic evidence on the subject. Arcesilas II ap-

---

19. Herodotus 4.160.
20. Chamoux, *Cyrène*, p. 218.
21. Herodotus 4.165.
22. Pindar *Pyth.* 5, 73ff.

Arcesilas Cup, ca. 560 B.C., courtesy of the Bibliothèque nationale, Paris

pears on the well known Arcesilas Cup,[23] painted by a Spartan artist ca. 560 B.C., and he is a figure of considerable majesty. Wearing a white tunic, and with a scepter in hand, he supervises the lading of some commodity, probably silphion (on which the prosperity of Cyrene depended), by men of slighter

23. Doubts have been expressed whether the Arcesilas on the cup is indeed the Cyrenaean _basileus_. But the Arcesilas depicted is certainly not a figure from mythology; and the suggestion that he is a commoner, perhaps a sixth-century wool merchant, is a desperate attempt to evade the obvious. The only other sixth-century personage depicted in vase painting was Croesus; see P. Arias and M. Hirmer, _A History of 1000 Years of Greek Vase Painting_ (New York: Harry N. Abrams, Inc., n.d.), p. 332. For a color reproduction of the cup see Arias and Hirmer, pl. 24.

stature. If Arcesilas II was impressive enough to be depicted on a cup—an honor bestowed on few individuals in their lifetime—he must surely have helped to make the title that he bore as prestigious as any in the political lexicon of sixth-century Greece. In the event, he did become too much like a king, and the reform of ca. 550 B.C. was intended to prevent another *basileus* from attaining such personal power.

The Archaic institution of the single, lifetime *basileia* survived in Cyrene until ca. 440 B.C., although in attenuated form. At approximately the same time that the Cyrenaeans abolished their *basileia,* the Argives seem to have replaced their *basileus* with a *probasileus* and a board of generals. Although the arrogance or incompetence of the individuals, Melantas and Arcesilas IV, may have provided the occasion for the political reforms, one must remember that from the sixth century onward the Greek states were disinclined to invest any individual with extraordinary power, even for a limited time. Undoubtedly it was their experience with tyranny that persuaded the Greeks to distribute power among members of annual boards or colleges. At any rate, the temper of the times was against the permanent and single *basileus,* and so far as we know the Cyrenaean and the Argive were the last of the species. Neither on Crete nor at Samos is an exclusive hereditary *basileus* attested for the fifth century, and Tarentum probably discontinued its *basileia* after the military debacle of ca. 473 B.C. By the time that Herodotus published his history, the single, lifetime *basileiai* were all things of the past.

The hereditary *basileis* of Archaic Greece—at Cyrene, Thera, Sparta, various Cretan *poleis,* Tarentum, Argos, and perhaps Samos and other *poleis*—may have been responsible for giving to the word *basileus* a more regal meaning than it had in the eighth century. With this new exclusiveness, it may be, the word was not too inappropriate to be applied to the real monarchs on the horizons of the sixth-century Greeks: Alcetas or Amyntas in Macedon, Amasis in Egypt, Nebuchadnezzar in Babylon, and Cyrus in Persia.

CHAPTER V   CONCLUSION

We have now examined the various institutions, words, and literary accounts that have been offered as evidence that the Geometric *poleis* were ruled by kings. We have seen, first of all, that the great majority of *poleis* did not claim to have had kings after the heroic period. To three *poleis* post-heroic dynasties were attributed, but in each case the attribution is by way of a kinglist composed, in the interest of chronography or of genealogical claims, late in the Classical or in the Hellenistic period. The word *basileus* was indeed very common in the epics of Homer and Hesiod. In this poetry, however, the word does not mean "king"; instead, it denotes a highborn leader who is regularly flanked by other highborn leaders. The various Archaic and Classical officials who held the title of *basileus* were just as much responsible magistrates as were archons and *prytaneis*. The one apparent distinction of the title *basileus* was its suitability for a hereditary magistracy, perhaps because from the beginning the word had connotations of high birth. Even the *basileiai* of Thera and Cyrene were not survivals of primitive monarchies, but Archaic parallels to the Spartan *basileia*. Far from serving as evidence that the Greek *poleis* were in Geometric times ruled by monarchs, the hereditary *basileis* of the Archaic period gave to the word *basileus* the connotations of exclusiveness that hitherto it had not had.

This study has one firm negative conclusion: during the Geometric period the Greek *poleis* were not ruled by kings. Undoubtedly the states of the Late Helladic III period were monarchies, but the monarchies must have ended when these large states broke apart. In the Geometric period weak monarchies seem to have been preserved in those Peloponnesian *ethnē* which, after a fashion, survived the breakdown of the old order: Achaea, Arcadia, Messenia, and Lacedaemon. At no time were there kings in the *poleis*, which after the Bronze Age emerged as autonomous states in the Argolid, the Isthmus, the Aegean islands, and the coast of Asia Minor. At Athens (which, like Sparta, was both a polis and the center of a large state that survived from Late Helladic times) it is perhaps possible that, as the legend of Codrus implies, a monarchic regime lasted until finally it fell victim to invaders, though in the end the invaders retired from Attica.

Our study has some positive implications concerning the government of a typical polis in the Dark Age. Removing the king from the conventional picture, we may replace him with a small circle of hereditary leaders, whom we can now identify as *basileis*. And presumably there was an assembly in which the *basileis* could, in the presence of the people, state their views on issues of concern to the community. Such may have been the regime that Homer assumed for the two *poleis* depicted on the shield of Achilles, or that Hesiod was still familiar with at the end of the eighth century. The Dark Age polis surely had no king; it probably had no magistrates. The fact that *basileus* rarely had an exclusive sense in Homeric and Hesiodic poetry suggests that the *basileia* as an exclusive magistracy, familiar in the Archaic and Classical periods, was not instituted until shortly before this poetry was composed. One must at least admit the probability that until ca. 750 B.C. the typical Greek polis had no chief magistrate.

It is therefore possible that even though there was no tidal shift from monarchy to aristocracy in the eighth century, the century was nonetheless a time of great change. It was apparently in the eighth century that those formal institutions and practices that are associated with the historical *poleis* were adopted: the assignment of electoral powers to an assembly of citizens, the gradation of political privileges on the basis of wealth, and the institution of a council and magistracies to be filled by men of the governing class. It may after all have been in the eighth century that aristocratic classes such as the Hippobotae and the Bacchiads, and that citizen classes such as the *Gamoroi* and *Homoioi*, were first demarcated. What such a formalized and organized regime replaced, however, was not a king, but the small circle of *basileis* that had led the polis since its emergence as an autonomous community.

SELECTED BIBLIOGRAPHY

The following list is limited to those works cited in the notes by short title.

Andreev, Juri. "Könige und Königsherrschaft in den Epen Homers." *Klio* 61 (1979): 361–84.

Bury, J. B., and Meiggs, Russell. *A History of Greece to the Death of Alexander.* New York: St. Martin's, 1975.

Busolt, Georg. *Griechische Geschichte bis zur Schlacht bei Chaeronea.* 2nd ed. Gotha: Perthes, 1893.

_____. *Griechische Staatskunde.* Vol. 1. Munich: Beck, 1920.

Catling, H. W. "Excavations at the Menelaion, Sparta, 1973–1976." *Arch. Rep. for 1976–1977,* no. 23, pp. 24–42.

Chamoux, François. *Cyrène sous la monarchie des Battiades.* Paris: Boccard, 1953.

Cook, J. M. "Early Greek Settlement in the Eastern Aegean and Asia Minor." *CAH*² II, 2, pp. 773–804.

Deger, Sigrid. *Herrschaftsformen bei Homer. Dissertationen der Universität Wien,* no. 43. Vienna: Verlag Notring, 1970.

Diehl, Ernst. *Anthologia Lyrica Graeca.* Vols. 1 and 2. Leipzig: Teubner, 1924–25.

Drews, Robert. "Argos and Argives in the *Iliad.*" *CP* 74 (1979): 111–35.

_____. "Phoenicians, Carthage and the Spartan *Eunomia.*" *AJP* 100 (*TEKMHPION. A Special Issue in Honor of James Henry Oliver.* 1979): 45–58.

Dunbabin, T. J. *The Western Greeks.* Oxford: Clarendon, 1948.

Forrest, W. G. *The Emergence of Greek Democracy 800–400 B.C.* New York: McGraw-Hill, 1966.

Graham, A. J. *Colony and Mother City in Ancient Greece.* New York: Barnes and Noble, Inc., 1964.

133

Grote, George. *A History of Greece.* 1849. Reprint in twelve volumes. New York: Dutton, 1906.

Gschnitzer, Fritz. "ΒΑΣΙΛΕΥΣ. Ein terminologischer Beitrag zur Frühgeschichte des Königtums bei den Griechen." *Innsbrucker Beiträge zur Kulturwissenschaft* 11 (1965): 99–112.

Huxley, G. L. *The Early Ionians.* London: Faber and Faber, 1966.

Jacoby, Felix. *Atthis. The Local Chronicles of Ancient Athens.* Oxford: Clarendon, 1949.

_____. *A Commentary on the Ancient Historians of Athens.* Leiden: Brill, 1954 (= *F.Gr.Hist.* Suppl. vols. 1 and 2).

Jeffery, Lillian. "The Courts of Justice in Archaic Chios." *ABSA* 51 (1956): 157–67.

_____. *The Local Scripts of Archaic Greece.* Oxford: Oxford Univ. Press, 1961.

_____. *Archaic Greece.* New York: St. Martin's, 1976.

Jones, W. H. S.; Ormerod, H. A.; and Wycherley, R. E., eds. *Pausanias. Description of Greece.* 5 vols. Cambridge and London: Harvard Univ. Press and Wm. Heinemann, 1918–1935.

Kelly, Thomas. *A History of Argos to 500 B.C.* Minneapolis: Univ. of Minnesota Press, 1976.

Kinkel, G. *Epicorum Graecorum Fragmenta.* Leipzig: Teubner, 1877.

Lejeune, M. "Les forgerons de Pylos." *Historia* 10 (1961): 409–34.

Lewis, D. M. *Sparta and Persia.* Leiden: Brill, 1977.

Meiggs, Russell, and Lewis, D. M. *A Selection of Greek Historical Inscriptions.* Oxford: Clarendon, 1969.

Merkelbach, R., and West, M. *Hesiodi Fragmenta Selecta* (bound with *Hesiodi Theogonia Opera et Dies Scutum,* ed. F. Solmsen). Oxford: Clarendon, 1970.

Meyer, Eduard. *Geschichte des Alterthums.* Vol. 2. 1st ed. Stuttgart: Cotta, 1893.

Mosshammer, Alden. *The Chronicle of Eusebius and Greek Chronographic Tradition.* Lewisburg, Pa.: Bucknell Univ. Press, 1979.

Oliva, Pavel. "ΠΑΤΡΙΚΗ ΒΑΣΙΛΕΙΑ." In *Geras. Studies Presented to George Thomson on the Occasion of his 60th Birthday,* edited by L. Varcl and R. F. Willetts, pp. 171–81. Prague: Charles Univ. Press, 1963.

Oost, S. I. "The Megara of Theagenes and Theognis." *CP* 68 (1973): 186–96.

Page, Denys. *History and the Homeric Iliad.* Berkeley: Univ. of California Press, 1959.

Pearson, Lionel. "The Pseudo-History of Messenia and its Authors." *Historia* 11 (1962): 397–426.

Sealey, Raphael. *A History of the Greek City States, 700–338 B.C.* Berkeley: Univ. of California Press, 1976.

Starr, Chester. "The Decline of the Early Greek Kings." *Historia* 10 (1961), pp. 129–38.

———. *The Economic and Social Growth of Early Greece 800–500 B.C.* New York: Oxford Univ. Press, 1977.

Thomas, C. G. "The Roots of Homeric Kingship." *Historia* 15 (1966): 387–407.

———. "From Wanax to Basileus: Kingship in the Greek Dark Age." *Hispania Antiqua* 6 (1978): 187–206.

Tomlinson, R. A. *Argos and the Argolid.* Ithaca: Cornell Univ. Press, 1972.

Wade-Gery, H. T. *The Poet of the Iliad.* Cambridge: Cambridge Univ. Press, 1952.

Webster, T. B. L. *From Mycenae to Homer.* 2nd ed. New York: Norton, 1964.

Will, Édouard. *Korinthiaka.* Paris: Boccard, 1955.

INDEX

Acastus, 88
Achaea, 42–43, 83
Achilles, 101, 103, 104
Aegina, 26, 27, 28, 86
Aeolic Greece, 6, 98
Aepytus of Arcadia, 72, 76, 78
Aepytus of Messenia, 75, 76, 77
Agamemnon, 1n2, 5–7, 9, 31, 57,
    101, 103–04
Agamemnon of Cyme, 32–35, 97
Agapenor, 72
Agariste, 61
Agiads, 82–84
Aisymnētēs, 18, 57
Alcaeus, 30, 107
Alcimus, 18n26
Alcinous, 105n17
Alcmaeonids, 11, 91
Aletes, 41, 46, 53, 54
Amphiclus, 21–22
Amphicrates, 27–28, 97
Amphidamas, 9
Amphitres, 17–18, 19–20
Anax, 102, 103, 104
Andraemon, 11, 15
Andreev, J., 3, 4, 99, 109–10, 112
Androclus, 11, 13, 14–15, 26
Antiochus the Heraclid, 49, 53
Antiochus of Syracuse, 53
Apaturia, 12
Apoikos, 16
Apollodorus, 52

Arcadia, 71–74, 93, 111
Arcesilas II, 126–28
Arcesilas IV, 128
Archagetēs, 85, 124
Archias, 39, 53
Archons, 87, 88, 91, 93, 101n8, 109,
    116, 117, 118; achonlist, 28, 89,
    90, 93, 97; decennial, 87–92
    passim
Areopagus, Council of the, 118
Argos, 58–71, 118, 120, 128
Aristodemus, 40, 41
Aristophilides, 36–38, 81, 97
Aristotle, 7, 37, 88, 119
Ascra, 106n21
Athenaion Politeia, 88–90
Athens, 5, 11–14, 22–23, 86–94,
    117, 118. See also Attica
Atthidographers, 90–91, 92
Attica, 111, 114, 130; as ethnos, 86

Bacchiads, 45–52, 120, 131
Bacchis, 49, 54
Basileis, college of, 35, 117; at
    Chios, 25–26; at Mytilene, 31; at
    Cyme, 34–35; at Elis, 41; at
    Athens, 117
Basileus
—as annual magistrate, 5, 63n,
    117–18, 120; at Chios, 25; at
    Megara, 56–57; at Chalcedon, 57;
    at Athens, 117–18

137